WORD PLAY

WHATZIT?™

UP & DOWN WORDS™

QUICKCROSS™

PLAY THESE OTHER FUN PUZZLE BOOKS BY USA TODAY:

USA TODAY SUDOKU

USA TODAY EVERYDAY SUDOKU

USA TODAY CROSSWORD

USA TODAY MINI SUDOKU / SUDOKU X

USA TODAY WORD ROUNDUP™ / WORD SEARCH

USA TODAY LOGIC PUZZLES

Word Play

WHATZIT?™

UP & DOWN WORDS™

QUICKCROSS™

200 PUZZLES

from The Nation's No. 1 Newspaper

Andrews McMeel
Publishing, LLC

Kansas City

 For information, write Andrews McMeel Publishing, LLC, an Andrews McMeel Universal company, 4520 Main Street, Kansas City, Missouri 64111.

07 08 09 10 11 BID 10 9 8 7 6 5 4 3 2 1

ISBN-13: 978-0-7407-7035-7
ISBN-10: 0-7407-7035-7

Distributed by Universal Press Syndicate
Up & Down Words by David L. Hoyt
QuickCross by John Wilmes

www.andrewsmcmeel.com
puzzles.usatoday.com

Introduction

Word puzzles are an entertaining way to flex your brain, relax, and take some time for yourself. This *USA TODAY* word puzzle collection offers three varieties of word puzzles: WHATZIT?, a word phrase game, Up & Down Words, a mix-and-match word clue game, and QuickCross, a mini crossword puzzle. These 200 challenging puzzles will be sure to sharpen your keen wordsmith skills!

WHATZIT?™

How to Play: Find the familiar phrase, saying, or name in the arrangement of letters.

SOLUTION: Checkered flag

Up & Down Words™

1	LIKE	NEW
2	NEW	MEXICO
3	MEXICO	
4		
5		
6		
7		CAPSULE

CLUES

1 As though never used
2 One of 50
3 A large metropolis
4 An Al Pacino film
5 _____ _____ Fame
6 The test _____ _____
7 Historical container

How to Play: The second word of each solution is the first word of the next solution.

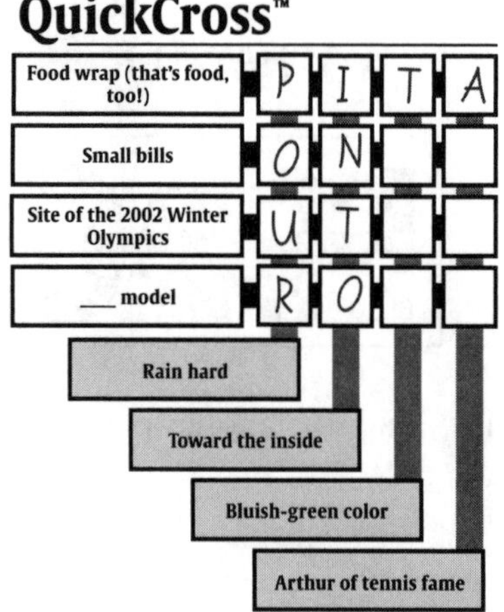

QuickCross™
Food wrap (that's food, too!)
P I T A
Small bills
O N
Site of the 2002 Winter Olympics
U T
___ model
R O
Rain hard
Toward the inside
Bluish-green color
Arthur of tennis fame

How to Play: QuickCross is a four-by-four crossword puzzle with eight word clues, four across and four down. The four-letter answers can be names, abbreviations, acronyms, prefixes, or even more than one word.

WHATZIT?™

1

Jail break

USA TODAY®

2

Holy Water

H_2OLY

3

weeping willow

PING WILLOW

4

thicket

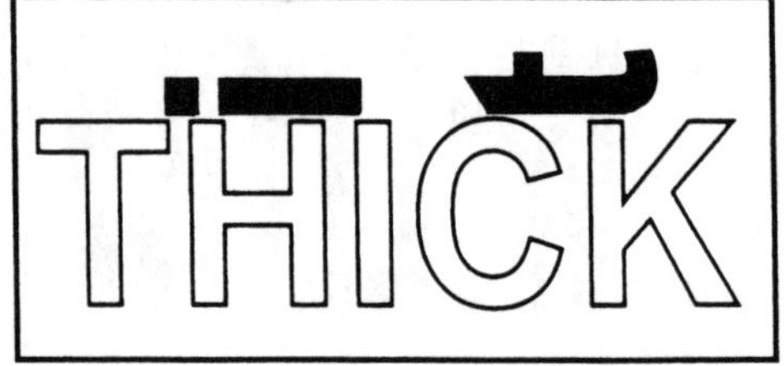

5

broken rib

6

eye shadow

WHATZIT?™

7

burst into tears

TIERBURSTTEAR

8

Ƨ□1

USA TODAY®

9

IT
IT
TONGUE

10

K9£

USA TODAY®

WHATZIT?™

brute force

BRUTE FOR FORE FOUR

12

13

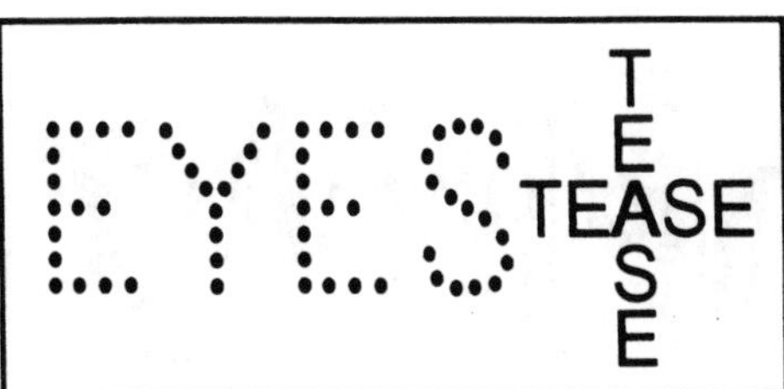

WHATZIT?™

14

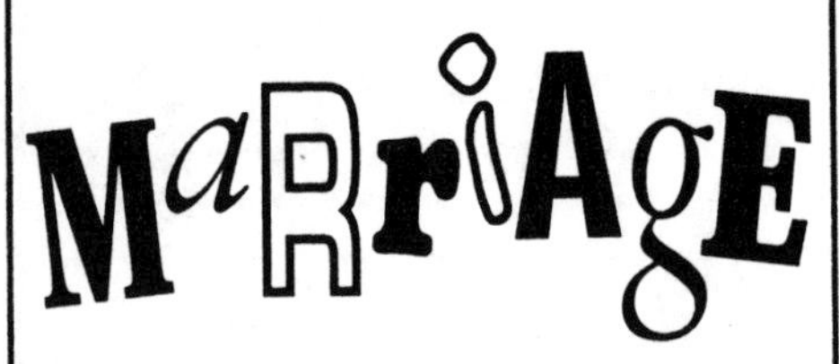

WHATZIT?™

15

win eee

16

17

P
FLASH
N

WHATZIT?™

18

UR
YO MIND

19

M ckey
M nn e
M ghty

20

QUEUE
READ
QUEUE

21

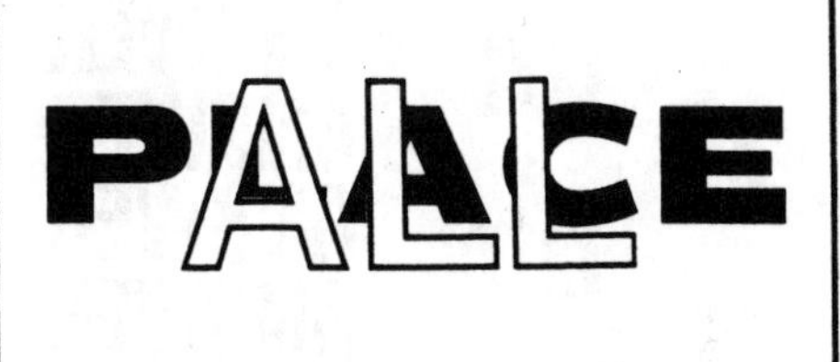

USA TODAY.

WHATZIT?™

22

	LOT	ANSWER
A		ANSWER
	LOT	ANSWER
		ANSWER

23

HO
HO
+HO

24

USA TODAY®

25

ADO	ADO	ADO	ADO	ADO	ADO	ADO
ADO	ADO	ADO	ADO	ADO	ADO	ADO
ADO	ADO				ADO	ADO
ADO	ADO				ADO	ADO
ADO	ADO				ADO	ADO
ADO	ADO	ADO	ADO	ADO	ADO	ADO
ADO	ADO	ADO	ADO	ADO	ADO	ADO

WHATZIT?™

26

SCOTLAND FEET FEET FEET

WHATZIT?™

27

TИƎVƎ TИƎVƎ

28

WELL	WELL	WELL	WELL
WELL	WELL	WELL	WELL
WELL	WELL	WELL	WELL
WELL	WELL	WELL	WELL
WELL	WELL	WELL	GOOD

29

gap gap

USA TODAY.

30

TRUTH

USA TODAY®

WHATZIT?™

31

DESPERATE
1 2 3 4

WHATZIT?™

32

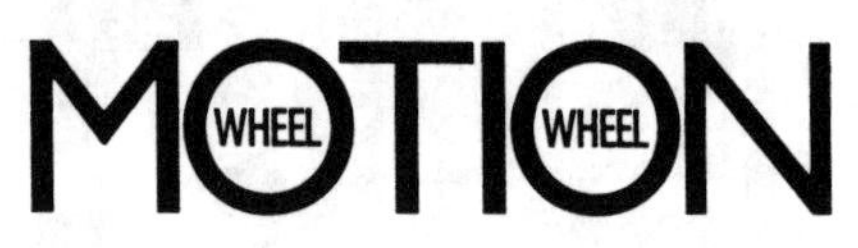

33

dijon

WHATZIT?™

34

razor #

35

36

GLIDING

WHATZIT?™

37

D E T A I L
D E T A I L

SATAN

38

C R Y S T A L

WHATZIT?™

39

won	won	
won		one
won	won	

WHATZIT?™

40

♀WW2♂

WHATZIT?™

41

ie Cexcept

42

E

UNIVERSE

O

M

43

Feet Feat
TERRA FIRMA

44

ATLAN**TA**
SEATT**LE**

WHATZIT?™

45

ROUND ROUND R
O
U
N
D

USA TODAY®

46

CASE

USA TODAY®

47

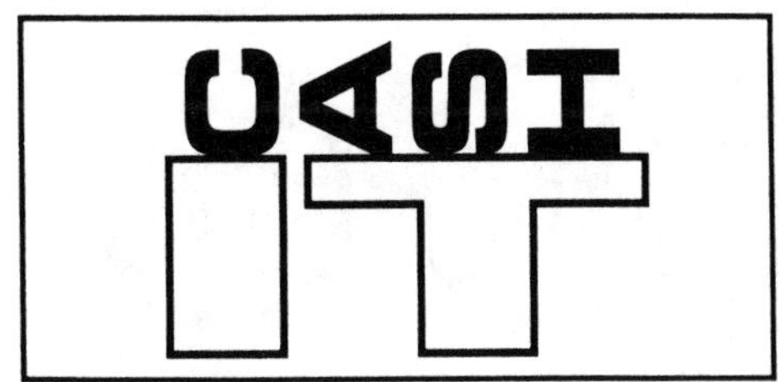

WHATZIT?™

48

49

WHATZIT?™

50

Through thick and thin

THROUGH

Up & Down Words™

1	CATCH	COLD
2	COLD	WINTER
3	WINTER	STORM
4	STORM	WARNING
5	WARNING	TRACK
6	TRACK	STAR
7	STAR	WARS

CLUES
1 Get the sniffles
2 Reason to bundle up a lot
3 A blizzard, for example
4 A reason to take cover
5 Part of a baseball field
6 Marion Jones, for example
7 1977 movie

52

Up & Down Words™

1	BLACK		BOX
2	BOX	↔	OFFICE
3	OFFICE	↔	
4		↔	COFFE
5	COFFEE	↔	BREAK
6	BREAK	↔	EVEN
7	EVEN	↔	PAR

CLUES

1 Flight recorder
2 Ticket sales area
3 Indoor business area
4 Orbiting laboratory
5 Type of pause
6 Bring in as much as you spend
7 A golfing term

53

Up & Down Words™

1 MENTAL ______ ______

2 ______ ______

3 ______ ______

4 ______ ______

5 ______ ______

6 ______ ______

7 ______ LICENSE

CLUES

1 Psychological fitness
2 Gym
3 A clear drink
4 A soft drink
5 This is usually easy to catch
6 An angling sport
7 Angler's permission slip

Up & Down Words™

1 NEXT ______ ______

2 ______ ______

3 ______ ______

4 ______ ______

5 ______ ______

6 ______ ______

7 ______ CRITIC

CLUES

1 Upcoming season of new growth
2 A May marriage, for example
3 Bride and groom's time period
4 Profession
5 A strike, for example
6 "Die Hard," for example
7 Certain reviewer

Up & Down Words™

1 NATIONAL ______ ↔ ______

2 ______ ↔ ______

3 ______ ↔ ______

4 ______ ↔ ______

5 ______ ↔ ______

6 ______ ↔ ______

7 ______ ↔ GRIMM

CLUES

1 A 2004 Nicholas Cage movie
2 Type of container
3 ____ ____ drawers
4 The test ____ ____
5 A large media company
6 A large movie studio
7 Famous siblings

56

Up & Down Words™

1 SULFURIC ______ ______

2 ______ ______

3 ______ ______

4 ______ ______

5 ______ ______

6 ______ ______

7 ______ RADIO

CLUES

1 A corrosive substance
2 Destructive precipitation
3 Important tropical area
4 A reason to call for help
5 A loud warning device
6 Something you can set
7 Bedside electronic device

Up & Down Words™

1 WONDER ______ ______

2 ______ ______

3 ______ ______

4 ______ ______

5 ______ ______

6 ______ ______

7 ______ LINE

CLUES

1 Question
2 Possible response to a vague question
3 Wrong
4 An intersection option
5 Go to bed
6 ____ ____ beginning...
7 "Walk ____ ____"

Up & Down Words™

1	HEAVY	
2		
3		
4		
5		
6		
7		PLACES

CLUES

1 A reason to get frustrated
2 A colorful signal
3 Wintertime precipitation
4 Something a student wants
5 24-hour break from your job
6 Deactivating lever
7 Change positions

Up & Down Words™

1 SEE		
2		
3		
4		
5		
6		
7		WINGS

CLUES

1 Become angry
2 Extremely warm
3 This can be poured into a mug
4 A piece of furniture
5 A food additive
6 Dead Sea liquid
7 Children's flotation devices

Up & Down Words™

1 NOT		
2	↔	
3	↔	
4	↔	
5	↔	
6	↔	
7	↔	SOUND

CLUES

1 Unamusing
2 It's found near the elbow
3 Parched
4 Trial, test
5 Deplete
6 Audibly
7 What thunder is

Up & Down Words™

1 THE __________ ↔ __________

2 __________ ↔ __________

3 __________ ↔ __________

4 __________ ↔ __________

5 __________ ↔ __________

6 __________ ↔ __________

7 __________ ↔ HOUSE

CLUES

1 Center
2 Standpoint between extremes
3 Type of chopped beef
4 Provision carrier
5 Settlers' column of vehicles
6 A type of hub
7 Police or fire department office

Up & Down Words™

1 NOT ______ ______

2 ______ ↔ ______

3 ______ ↔ ______

4 ______ ↔ ______

5 ______ ↔ ______

6 ______ ↔ ______

7 ______ ↔ BOY

CLUES

1 Erroneous
2 Loyal
3 Clear day's view
4 Way up in the air
5 English afternoon break
6 Small, porous sack
7 A grocery store worker

63

Up & Down Words™

1 GROW ______ ______

2 ______ ______

3 ______ ______

4 ______ ______

5 ______ ______

6 ______ ______

7 ______ PIGEON

CLUES

1 Age
2 "This ___ ___" (TV show)
3 Type of access provider
4 You might keep one in your pocket
5 Circulating correspondence
6 Mailman
7 Flying deliverer

Up & Down Words™

1 VENOMOUS ______ ______

2 ______ ↔ ______

3 ______ ↔ ______

4 ______ ↔ ______

5 ______ ↔ ______

6 ______ ↔ ______

7 ______ ↔ DOORS

CLUES

1 A tarantula, for example
2 A tropical primate
3 Shenanigans
4 Money-making agenda
5 ____ ____ attack
6 King ____ ____ hill
7 1991 Val Kilmer movie

Up & Down Words™

1 COURT ______ ↔ ______
2 ______ ↔ ______
3 ______ ↔ ______
4 ______ ↔ ______
5 ______ ↔ ______
6 ______ ↔ ______
7 ______ ↔ MILLS

CLUES
1 Type of military trial
2 It's instituted in a time of crisis
3 Attorney's institution
4 Educational precinct
5 A type of lawyer
6 Chief law officer
7 A large cereal maker

Up & Down Words™

1 AT ____________ ____________

2 ____________ ↔ ____________

3 ____________ ↔ ____________

4 ____________ ↔ ____________

5 ____________ ↔ ____________

6 ____________ ↔ ____________

7 ____________ ↔ CAR

CLUES

1 In the beginning
2 A Sylvester Stallone movie
3 Red ____ ____
4 Type of communication device
5 Directory
6 Oprah's literary collective
7 Part of a train

67

Up & Down Words™

1 *SNOW* ______ ______

2 ______ ______

3 ______ ______

4 ______ ______

5 ______ ______

6 ______ ______

7 ______ *AHEAD*

CLUES

1 A fictional female
2 A famous home
3 Mobile home
4 Mobile home area
5 The U.S. National ___ ___
6 Type of extra fee
7 Move forward aggressively

Up & Down Words™

1	AT		
2		↔	
3		↔	
4		↔	
5		↔	
6		↔	
7		↔	SUPPLIES

CLUES
1 Finally
2 A bartender statement
3 Cancel
4 Unprepared
5 A security position
6 Mail center
7 Stapler, paper, etc.

Up & Down Words™

1 PRIVATE ________

2 ________ ________

3 ________ ________

4 ________ ________

5 ________ ________

6 ________ ________

7 ________ NUMBER

CLUES

1 Personal real estate
2 Type of real estate levy
3 Wealth within a jurisdiction
4 Reason to head to first
5 Listing of popular songs
6 Ceremonial display path
7 66, for example

70

Up & Down Words™

1	SUDDEN	
2		
3		
4		
5		
6		
7		OUT

CLUES

1 ____ ____ playoff
2 Type of sentence
3 A soccer player can take one
4 A rough sport
5 Bout
6 A tennis term
7 Bring attention to

Up & Down Words™

1 DAILY ______ ↔ ______

2 ______ ↔ ______

3 ______ ↔ ______

4 ______ ↔ ______

5 ______ ↔ ______

6 ______ ↔ ______

7 ______ ↔ PROGRAM

CLUES

1 A pair of races
2 A baseball term
3 Fun period for kids
4 Break
5 In poor taste
6 Type of set
7 Show

Up & Down Words™

1	FRANKFORT	________
2	________	________
3	________	________
4	________	________
5	________	________
6	________	________
7	________	OPENER

CLUES
1 A U.S. state capital
2 ____ ____ Chicken
3 Type of cooked mollusk
4 Sea creature housing
5 A large petroleum company
6 Type of container
7 Used to get into a container

73

Up & Down Words™

1 EXTRA ______ ↔ ______

2 ______ ↔ ______

3 ______ ↔ ______

4 ______ ↔ ______

5 ______ ↔ ______

6 ______ ↔ ______

7 ______ ↔ MOUTH

CLUES

1 Very big
2 Big clan
3 Genealogy
4 Type of limb
5 Expand
6 Audibly
7 Obnoxious talker

Up & Down Words™

1 TURNING ______ ______

2 ______ ↔ ______

3 ______ ↔ ______

4 ______ ↔ ______

5 ______ ↔ ______

6 ______ ↔ ______

7 ______ ↔ THE ______

CLUES

1 Time of significant change
2 ____ ____ sale
3 A matter ____ ____
4 A popular publication
5 Place to buy a publication
6 "____ ____ Me" (movie)
7 ____ ____ book

75

Up & Down Words™

1 FRESH ____ ↔ ____

2 ____ ↔ ____

3 ____ ↔ ____

4 ____ ↔ ____

5 ____ ↔ ____

6 ____ ↔ ____

7 ____ ↔ POLE

CLUES

1 This is clean and breathable
2 Certain pocket of gas
3 Something that is chewed
4 You should brush around yours
5 What to do at a busy checkout stand
6 The Arctic's locale
7 Cold top

76

Up & Down Words™

1	MEXICAN	
2		
3		
4		
5		
6		
7		UP

CLUES

1 Four U.S. states touch this
2 Protector of the perimeter
3 Assignment to be on the lookout
4 An airport shop
5 Type of present
6 Cover with paper and bow
7 Bring to a close

77

Up & Down Words™

1	TOM	
2		
3		
4		
5		
6		
7		EYE

CLUES

1 A fictional character
2 You can leave one as evidence
3 A key on most keyboards
4 AOL members have one
5 Sometimes found on a car or door
6 Type of transparent sheet
7 Peter Falk has one

Up & Down Words™

1 *BAKING* ______ ↔ ______

2 ______ ↔ ______

3 ______ ↔ ______

4 ______ ↔ ______

5 ______ ↔ ______

6 ______ ↔ ______

7 ______ ↔ *DEALER*

CLUES

1 Sodium bicarbonate
2 Mountain Dew, for example
3 A style of tunes
4 A band can make one
5 Blockbuster's service
6 Automobile used for a short time
7 Automobile seller

79

Up & Down Words™

1	CHEMICAL	
2		
3		
4		
5		
6		
7		IT

CLUES

1 Type of response
2 Duration until a response
3 Test race
4 ____ ____ error
5 Most definitely
6 "____ ____ that sound?"
7 Easy ____ ____

Up & Down Words™

1 FIREWORKS ________ ________

2 ________ ________

3 ________ ________

4 ________ ________

5 ________ ________

6 ________ ________

7 ________ CALL

CLUES

1 A "Fourth" exhibition
2 Transparent or open cabinet
3 ___ ___ point
4 ___ ___ deep
5 What a pity
6 Reason to stay home from work
7 Salesperson's option

Up & Down Words™

1 BEAT ______ ↔ ______

2 ______ ↔ ______

3 ______ ↔ ______

4 ______ ↔ ______

5 ______ ↔ ______

6 ______ ↔ ______

7 ______ ↔ BOSS

CLUES

1 "____ ____ Clock" (TV show)
2 A Peter Benchley novel
3 Alabama's locale
4 A former country
5 This ended in 1975
6 Illegal military offense
7 Mafia figure

82

Up & Down Words™

1	GOOD		
2		↔	
3		↔	
4		↔	
5		↔	
6		↔	
7		↔	EFFORT

CLUES

1 TV show set in Chicago
2 NYC landmark
3 Prepare to fight
4 "Better ____ ____" (movie)
5 Lifeless male
6 The Blue ____ ____
7 Cumulative attempt

83

Up & Down Words™

1 NOT ____________ ____________

2 ____________ ↔ ____________

3 ____________ ↔ ____________

4 ____________ ↔ ____________

5 ____________ ↔ ____________

6 ____________ ↔ ____________

7 ____________ ↔ FACT

CLUES
1 Difficult
2 Simple profit
3 Grasping device for bills
4 Attach
5 "Baby ____ ____"
6 ____ ____ trade or education
7 Matter ____ ____

Up & Down Words™

1 DRAG ________ ________

2 ________ ________

3 ________ ________

4 ________ ________

5 ________ ________

6 ________ ________

7 ________ MANNERS

CLUES
1 Speedy competition
2 A fast vehicle
3 Changing the oil, for example
4 Attend to
5 "What's ____ ____?"
6 Piece of furniture with chairs
7 Eater's good behavior

Up & Down Words™

1	DEEP	
2		
3		
4		
5		
6		
7		TO

CLUES

1 Needed for a dive
2 A child's toy
3 Bullet compartment
4 Played by a small ensemble
5 Tune-playing device
6 Put into a package
7 ____ ____ the minute

Up & Down Words™

1 LOOK ______ ______
2 ______ ______
3 ______ ______
4 ______ ______
5 ______ ______
6 ______ ______
7 ______ WARS

CLUES
1 View
2 On the loose
3 A St. Bernard, for example
4 A backyard structure, for some
5 Type of visitor
6 Special performer
7 A 1977 movie

Up & Down Words™

1	PRIME		
2		↔	
3		↔	
4		↔	
5		↔	
6		↔	
7		↔	PUT

CLUES

1 1, 2 or 3, for example
2 February or Venus
3 Nickname for $2,000
4 Type of hit
5 Easy thing's designation
6 A basketball term
7 An athletic event

Up & Down Words™

1 TABLE ________ ________

2 ________ ________

3 ________ ________

4 ________ ________

5 ________ ________

6 ________ ________

7 ________ OFF

CLUES

1 A food additive
2 Very abundant liquid
3 An Asian animal
4 William Fredrick Cody
5 Popular comedic actor
6 "The ____ ____" (TV show)
7 Display proudly

89

Up & Down Words™

1	TERM		
2		↔	
3		↔	
4		↔	
5		↔	
6		↔	
7		↔	OFF

CLUES

1 Type of document
2 "The ____ ____" (movie/TV show)
3 Run after
4 ____ ____ cookin'
5 It's played against a visitor
6 Intense, competitive look
7 Cool game's beginning

Up & Down Words™

1 JACK ______ ______

2 ______ ______

3 ______ ______

4 ______ ______

5 ______ ______

6 ______ ______

7 ______ OPENER

CLUES

1 "Shallow Hal" star
2 Found in some pens
3 Printer designation
4 Type of propulsion system
5 Type of lubricant
6 Lubricant container
7 Lid remover

91

Up & Down Words™

1 *TOO* ________ ↙↗ ________

2 ________ ↙↗ ________

3 ________ ↙↗ ________

4 ________ ↙↗ ________

5 ________ ↙↗ ________

6 ________ ↙↗ ________

7 ________ ↙↗ *CARES*

CLUES

1 Larger than desired
2 Important person
3 Small vessel for liquid
4 "Columbo" star has one
5 Ophthalmologist
6 British sci-fi show
7 Used like "whatever"

Up & Down Words™

1	ANOTHER	
2		
3		
4		
5		
6		
7		LETTER

CLUES
1 Further inspection
2 Good street-crossing advice
3 Initial filming
4 Seize control
5 Completed
6 Used like "affectionately yours"
7 Affectional correspondence

93

Up & Down Words™

1 JUNIOR ______ ______

2 ______ ______

3 ______ ______

4 ______ ______

5 ______ ______

6 ______ ______

7 ______ SEARCH

CLUES

1 Type of school
2 A track-and-field event
3 Way to enter a pool
4 Hole ___ ___
5 Eventually
6 Career
7 Employment hunt

94

Up & Down Words™

1 BIG ______ ______

2 ______ ↔ ______

3 ______ ↔ ______

4 ______ ↔ ______

5 ______ ↔ ______

6 ______ ↔ ______

7 ______ ↔ MECHANISM

CLUES

1 Goes with an exaggerate ego
2 Walk toward the Arctic
3 Iceland's location
4 Found east of "eastern"
5 Longitudinal division
6 A basketball term
7 Unconscious response

Up & Down Words™

1 *HIGHWAY* ______

2 ______ ______

3 ______ ______

4 ______ ______

5 ______ ______

6 ______ ______

7 ______ *GATES*

CLUES

1 "CHiPs" H and P
2 Police vehicle
3 Group of commuters
4 Chlorinated $H2O$
5 Heavyset mammal
6 Old West character
7 A rich, generous man

Up & Down Words™

1 NOT ______ ______

2 ______ ↔ ______

3 ______ ↔ ______

4 ______ ↔ ______

5 ______ ↔ ______

6 ______ ↔ ______

7 ______ ↔ BONE

CLUES

1 Nearby
2 Home to the Orient
3 Boston's shoreline region
4 Shoreline protectors
5 Alert canine
6 Worn by some canines
7 Clavicle

Up & Down Words™

1 *PRIVATE* ______ ↔ ______

2 ______ ↔ ______

3 ______ ↔ ______

4 ______ ↔ ______

5 ______ ↔ ______

6 ______ ↔ ______

7 ______ ↔ *DANCING*

CLUES

1 Exclusive organization
2 A clear drink
3 Coke or Pepsi, for example
4 Easily caught by an outfielder
5 Angling sport
6 Angler's cord
7 Done to country music

Up & Down Words™

1	LIVING	
2		
3		
4		
5		
6		
7		SLICK

CLUES

1 George Romero's stiffs in 1968
2 European low spot
3 Water-loving mammal
4 "The ____ ____" (movie)
5 Slithering reptile
6 Bogus medicine
7 Result of an accident at sea

99

Up & Down Words™

1 DIE ____________ ____________

2 ____________ ____________

3 ____________ ____________

4 ____________ ____________

5 ____________ ____________

6 ____________ ____________

7 ____________ PLAN

CLUES

1 1988 movie
2 Computer storage mechanism
3 ____ ____ theater
4 Together, with
5 Resign
6 You can put one on a house
7 Schedule of checks to write

Up & Down Words™

1 NOT ______ ______

2 ______ ______

3 ______ ______

4 ______ ______

5 ______ ______

6 ______ ______

7 ______ GAMES

CLUES

1 Untrue
2 Bye
3 Deep toss by a QB
4 Faint
5 ____ ____ control
6 Tug ____ ____
7 Combative exercises

101

Up & Down Words™

1 *BLUE* ______ ↔ ______

2 ______ ↔ ______

3 ______ ↔ ______

4 ______ ↔ ______

5 ______ ↔ ______

6 ______ ↔ ______

7 ______ ↔ *TV*

CLUES

1 Seen on a clear day
2 Way up in the air
3 Manufactured excellently
4 Craftsmanship check
5 Base of operations
6 Jump ball area
7 A cable network

Up & Down Words™

1 GIVE ______ ↔ ______

2 ______ ↔ ______

3 ______ ↔ ______

4 ______ ↔ ______

5 ______ ↔ ______

6 ______ ↔ ______

7 ______ ↔ TAGS

CLUES

1 Relinquish
2 Very near
3 Near miss
4 Cancel
5 Unready
6 Four-legged watcher
7 Used as identifiers

Up & Down Words™

1 ABSOLUTE ______

2 ______ ______

3 ______ ______

4 ______ ______

5 ______ ______

6 ______ ______

7 ______ CHANGE

CLUES

1 As cold as it gets
2 Focus toward, center on
3 Eventually
4 Order of events
5 ____ ____ fire or sight
6 Yes, certainly
7 Alteration of route

Up & Down Words™

1 ALL

2

3

4

5

6

7 BAGS

CLUES

1 Finished
2 Doomed
3 ____ ____ sign
4 Reduced cost
5 "The ____ ____ Right"
6 Time ____ ____
7 Rich person's nickname

Up & Down Words™

1 VERY ______ ______

2 ______ ↔ ______

3 ______ ↔ ______

4 ______ ↔ ______

5 ______ ↔ ______

6 ______ ↔ ______

7 ______ ↔ GO

CLUES

1 Extremely rotten
2 Misbehaving canine
3 Canine treat
4 Without any liquid
5 Lose moisture
6 ____ ____ lunch
7 Carryout

Up & Down Words™

1 NOT ____________ ↔ ____________

2 ____________ ↔ ____________

3 ____________ ↔ ____________

4 ____________ ↔ ____________

5 ____________ ↔ ____________

6 ____________ ↔ ____________

7 ____________ ↔ BEATLES

CLUES

1 Unjust
2 Decent charge
3 This is good for consumers
4 Military makeup
5 ____ ____ numbers
6 ____ ____ book
7 Famous foursome

107

Up & Down Words™

1 SPENDING ____________ ____________

2 ____________ ↔ ____________

3 ____________ ↔ ____________

4 ____________ ↔ ____________

5 ____________ ↔ ____________

6 ____________ ↔ ____________

7 ____________ ↔ KING

CLUES

1 Cash you can part with
2 ____ ____ guarantee
3 Accumulate in a congested area
4 The Arctic's locale
5 Often stormy body of water
6 Type of seal
7 "The ____ ____" (movie)

108

Up & Down Words™

1 TRY ______ ______
2 ______ ______
3 ______ ______
4 ______ ______
5 ______ ______
6 ______ ______
7 ______ OUT

CLUES

1 Make a good effort
2 ____ ____ Cafe
3 Played by the Stones
4 Ornamental tune player
5 Fun flyer
6 Flying cord
7 Make something continue

Up & Down Words™

1 NO ________ ________

2 ________ ________

3 ________ ________

4 ________ ________

5 ________ ________

6 ________ ________

7 ________ RACE

CLUES

1 Bad
2 Skillful grab
3 Get the sniffles
4 A weather term
5 Part of a car
6 Fun vehicle
7 Stock ____ ____

Up & Down Words™

1 BIG ________ ________

2 ________ ________

3 ________ ________

4 ________ ________

5 ________ ________

6 ________ ________

7 ________ SCOUT

CLUES
1 A circus area
2 Hush-hush
3 Classified cipher
4 Secret designation
5 "____ ____ Tune"
6 A Marlo Thomas sitcom
7 ____ ____ Cookies

Up & Down Words™

1 HELP ______ ______

2 ______ ______

3 ______ ______

4 ______ ______

5 ______ ______

6 ______ ______

7 ______ BOTTLE

CLUES

1 It's said to get assistance
2 Phrase of agreement
3 Skinnier than wanted
4 You don't want to be on this
5 A cold food
6 A sweet carbonated drink
7 Type of beverage container

Up & Down Words™

1	NOT	
2		
3		
4		
5		
6		
7		BASE

CLUES
1 Untrue
2 "Bye!"
3 Tiring 24 hours
4 Sunlit sporting event
5 Competitive program
6 Display proudly
7 Wrong, mistaken

Up & Down Words™

1 VOICE ______ ↔ ______

2 ______ ↔ ______

3 ______ ↔ ______

4 ______ ↔ ______

5 ______ ↔ ______

6 ______ ↔ ______

7 ______ ↔ LESSON

CLUES

1 Larynx
2 A long-lived reptile
3 A delicacy for some
4 Type of food provider
5 You can put a plate on one
6 A fast-paced sport
7 A reason to get a racket

114

Up & Down Words™

1 SALVATION ________ ________

2 ________ ________

3 ________ ________

4 ________ ________

5 ________ ________

6 ________ ________

7 ________ CALL

CLUES

1 A charitable group
2 Military installation
3 Minimum compensation
4 Compensation increase
5 Lift
6 Very near
7 Narrow escape

Up & Down Words™

1	STEPHEN		
2			
3			
4			
5			
6			
7			BARRIER

CLUES
1 "It" author
2 Brightly marked reptile
3 Place of chaotic disorder
4 Driver's break
5 Reason to put on the brakes
6 A form of communication
7 A communication obstacle

Up & Down Words™

1 NOT ______ ______

2 ______ ↔ ______

3 ______ ↔ ______

4 ______ ↔ ______

5 ______ ↔ ______

6 ______ ↔ ______

7 ______ ↔ DEFENSE

CLUES
1 Out
2 On the shelf, available
3 Type of trading arena
4 The result of supply and demand
5 A battle that's good for buyers
6 Battle sector
7 A basketball term

Up & Down Words™

1 WILD ________ ________

2 ________ ↔ ________

3 ________ ↔ ________

4 ________ ↔ ________

5 ________ ↔ ________

6 ________ ↔ ________

7 ________ ↔ AWAY

CLUES

1 A lion found in nature is one
2 Very large group of creatures
3 The next world
4 "Lassie ____ ____" (movie)
5 Take-____ ____
6 Reimburse
7 Retreat without turning around

Up & Down Words™

1 *EXTRA* ________ ________
2 ________ ↙↗ ________
3 ________ ↙↗ ________
4 ________ ↙↗ ________
5 ________ ↙↗ ________
6 ________ ↙↗ ________
7 ________ ↙↗ *GUARD*

CLUES
1 Optional assignment
2 It's usually made of plastic
3 Gin rummy, for example
4 A tennis term
5 1991 Keanu Reeves movie
6 Detach
7 Unprepared

119

Up & Down Words™

1 CHRIS ________ ________

2 ________ ________

3 ________ ________

4 ________ ________

5 ________ ________

6 ________ ________

7 ________ WELL

CLUES

1 Former "SNL" star
2 Chunky NaCl
3 Great ____ ____
4 One of five
5 A North American province
6 Ginger ale maker
7 Type of hole in the ground

120

Up & Down Words™

1 BAD	
2	
3	
4	
5	
6	
7	SCORE

CLUES
1 Canine scolding
2 Enclosure for strays
3 U.K. monetary unit
4 Type of alloy
5 Motion picture nickname
6 Type of audition
7 100 or A, for example

Up & Down Words™

1 LIMITED ______ ⤢ ______

2 ______ ⤢ ______

3 ______ ⤢ ______

4 ______ ⤢ ______

5 ______ ⤢ ______

6 ______ ⤢ ______

7 ______ ⤢ LIME

CLUES

1 Finite period
2 Interruption of chronological flow
3 Enterprise term
4 A reason to slow down
5 Kill
6 Varying from the proper pitch
7 ____ ____ pie

Up & Down Words™

1 DR.		
2		
3		
4		
5		
6		
7		COLD

CLUES

1 1962 movie
2 Bad
3 Attitude of friendliness
4 Actor born in Philadelphia
5 ____ ____ Wesson
6 In ____ ____
7 Unconscious

123

Up & Down Words™

1 TOM ______ ______
2 ______ ______
3 ______ ______
4 ______ ______
5 ______ ______
6 ______ ______
7 ______ UP

CLUES
1 Actor born in Syracuse
2 Type of large vessel
3 Leave
4 ____ ____ order
5 The speed ____ ____
6 Bright display
7 Arrive

Up & Down Words™

1 EASTER ______ ______

2 ______ ______

3 ______ ______

4 ______ ______

5 ______ ______

6 ______ ______

7 ______ PAL

CLUES

1 Rapa Nui
2 Japan, for example
3 A likely place to find a golf course
4 A carbonated beverage
5 Old-fashioned ice cream parlor
6 Writing instrument
7 A buddy to write to

Up & Down Words™

1	PRIVATE	
2		
3		
4		
5		
6		
7		MOUTH

CLUES
1 Exclusive land
2 It's paid to a local government
3 Tariff reduction
4 Reduce
5 Withdraw
6 Audibly
7 An obnoxious talker has one

126

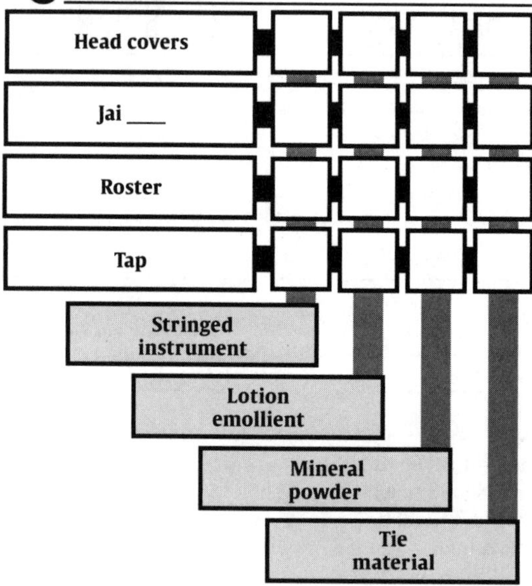
QuickCross™
Head covers
Jai ____
Roster
Tap
Stringed instrument
Lotion emollient
Mineral powder
Tie material

USA TODAY

QuickCross™

Across				
"For Sale" sign addendum				
Surface amount				
Close				
Completely cooked				

Beach basis

Cookie classic

Tend toward

Challenge

QuickCross™

Carefulness (Shortened?)

Comply

Not one (Shortened?)

Alphabetic animals?

Ice-cream supporter?

"Bravo! Take _ ___!"

Ms. Russo

They look out for you?

129

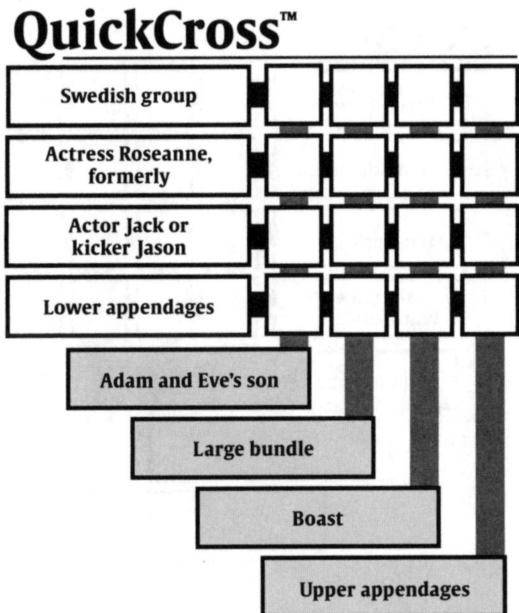
QuickCross™
Swedish group
Actress Roseanne, formerly
Actor Jack or kicker Jason
Lower appendages
Adam and Eve's son
Large bundle
Boast
Upper appendages

USA TODAY

130

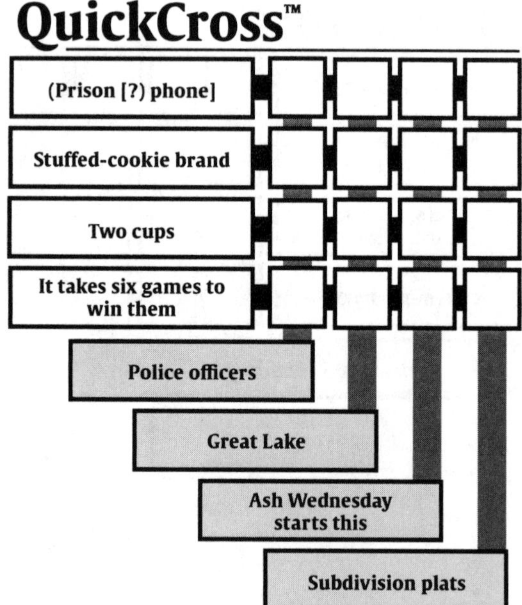
QuickCross™
(Prison [?) phone]
Stuffed-cookie brand
Two cups
It takes six games to win them
Police officers
Great Lake
Ash Wednesday starts this
Subdivision plats

USA TODAY

131

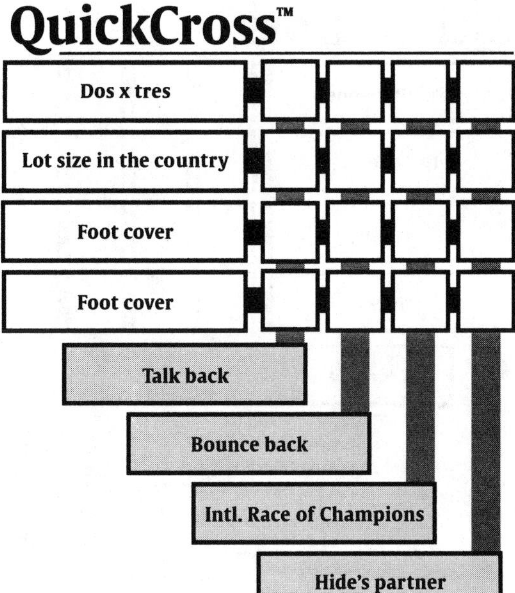
QuickCross™
Dos x tres
Lot size in the country
Foot cover
Foot cover
Talk back
Bounce back
Intl. Race of Champions
Hide's partner

USA TODAY

132

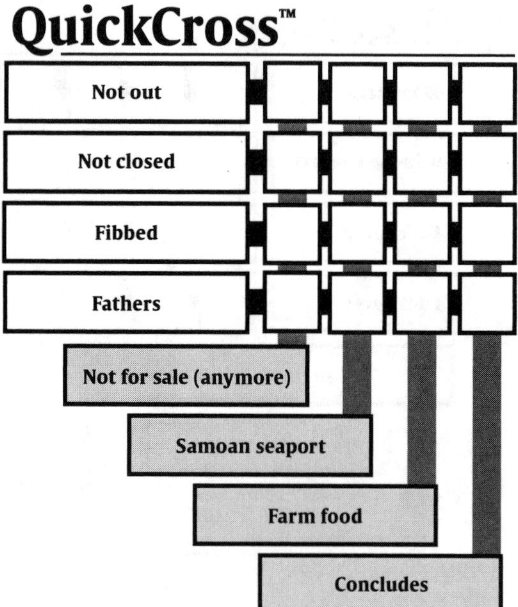
QuickCross™
Not out
Not closed
Fibbed
Fathers
Not for sale (anymore)
Samoan seaport
Farm food
Concludes

USA TODAY

133

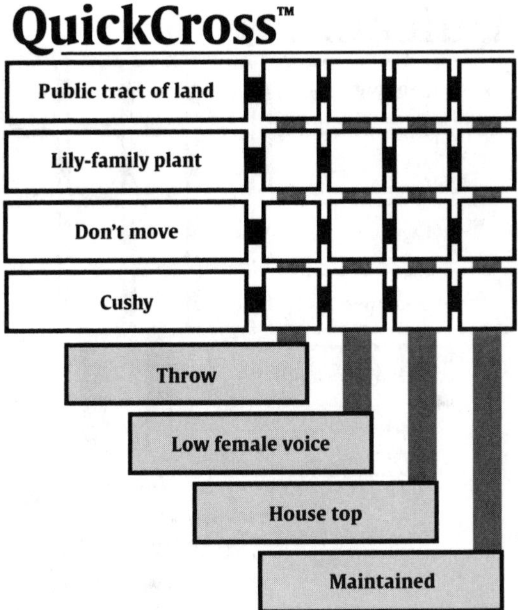
QuickCross™
Public tract of land
Lily-family plant
Don't move
Cushy
Throw
Low female voice
House top
Maintained

USA TODAY

134

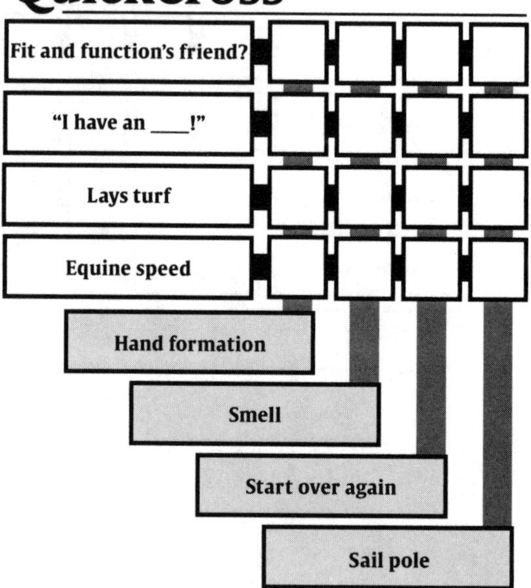
QuickCross™
Fit and function's friend?
"I have an ____!"
Lays turf
Equine speed
Hand formation
Smell
Start over again
Sail pole

USA TODAY®

135

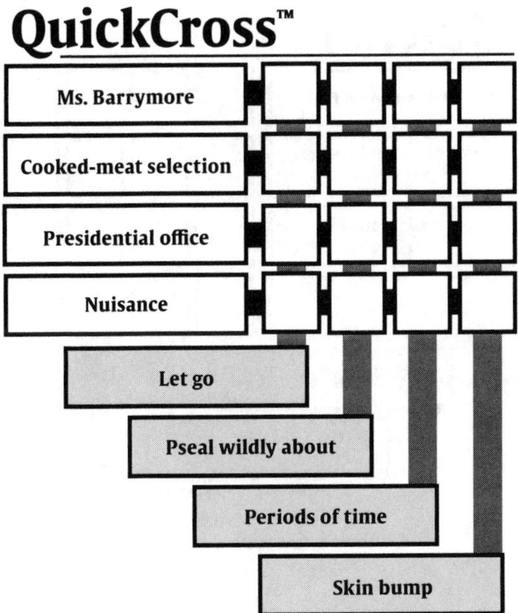
QuickCross™
Ms. Barrymore
Cooked-meat selection
Presidential office
Nuisance
Let go
Pseal wildly about
Periods of time
Skin bump

USA TODAY.

136

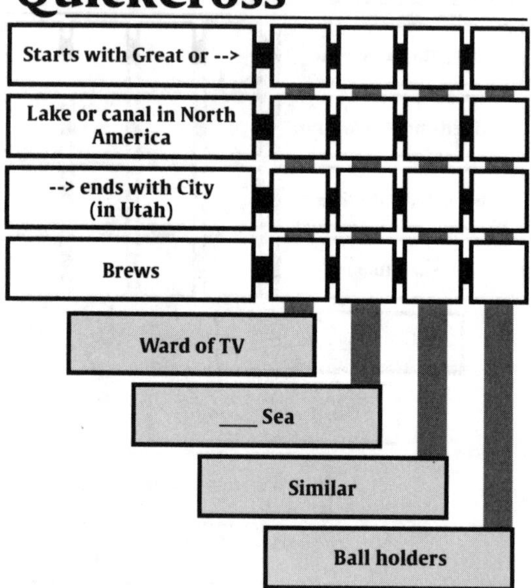
QuickCross™
Starts with Great or -->
Lake or canal in North America
--> ends with City (in Utah)
Brews
Ward of TV
___ Sea
Similar
Ball holders

USA TODAY.

137

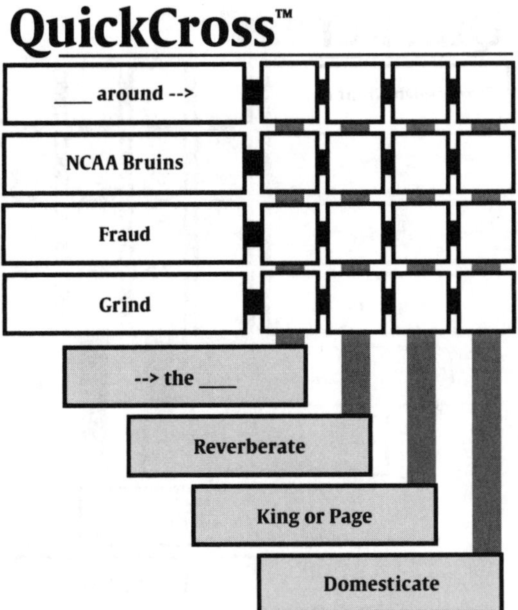
QuickCross™
___ around -->
NCAA Bruins
Fraud
Grind
--> the ___
Reverberate
King or Page
Domesticate

USA TODAY.

QuickCross™

Japanese liquor				
Drafty				
Adhesive				
Requests				

Tale

Suffers

Former Phillie John

Hurricane hearts

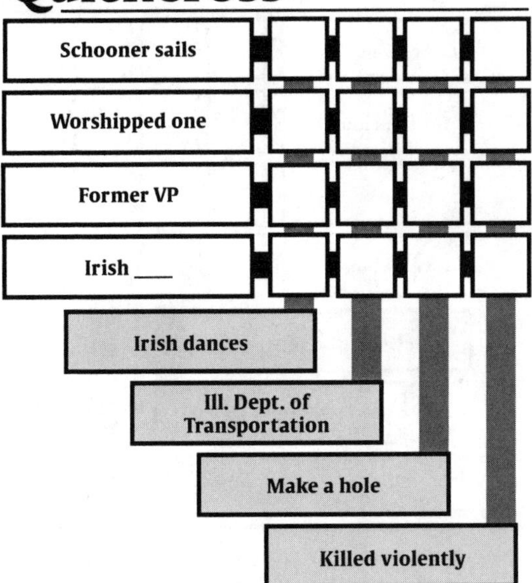
QuickCross™
Schooner sails
Worshipped one
Former VP
Irish ___
Irish dances
Ill. Dept. of Transportation
Make a hole
Killed violently

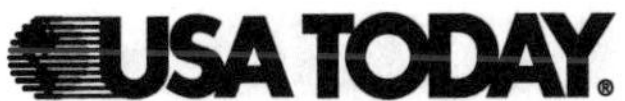
USA TODAY®

140

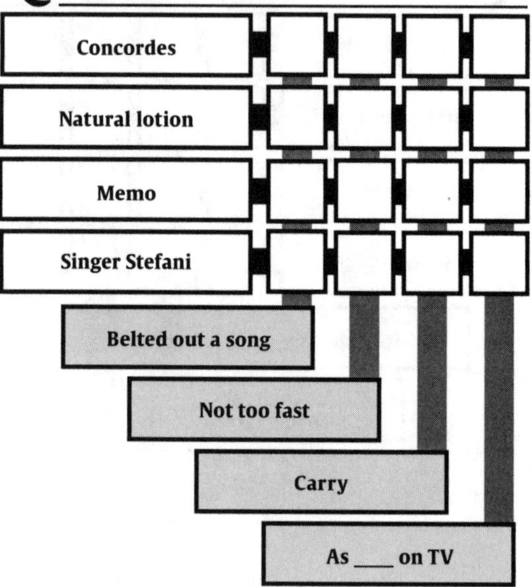
QuickCross™
Concordes
Natural lotion
Memo
Singer Stefani
Belted out a song
Not too fast
Carry
As ____ on TV

USA TODAY®

141

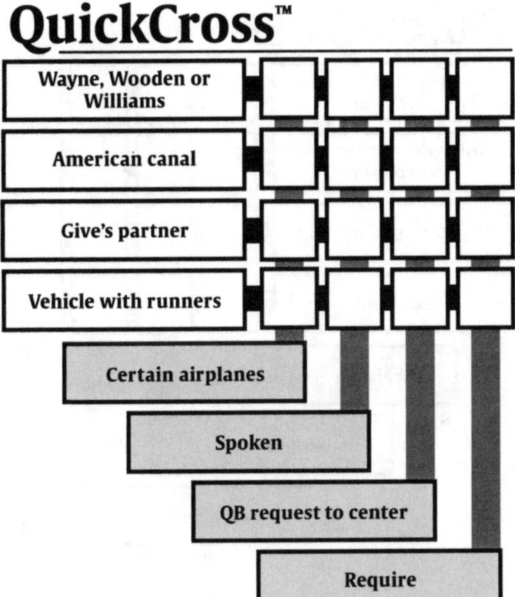
QuickCross™
Wayne, Wooden or Williams
American canal
Give's partner
Vehicle with runners
Certain airplanes
Spoken
QB request to center
Require

USA TODAY®

142

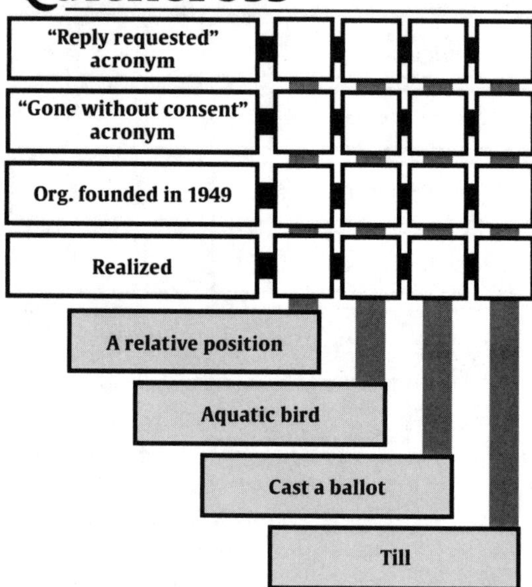
QuickCross™
"Reply requested" acronym
"Gone without consent" acronym
Org. founded in 1949
Realized
A relative position
Aquatic bird
Cast a ballot
Till

USA TODAY

QuickCross™

Across				
Acquire				
Slender instrument				
Elbow-to-wrist bone				
Trial				

Down:

- Constitutional disease
- Capable
- Charged atoms
- Orderly

144

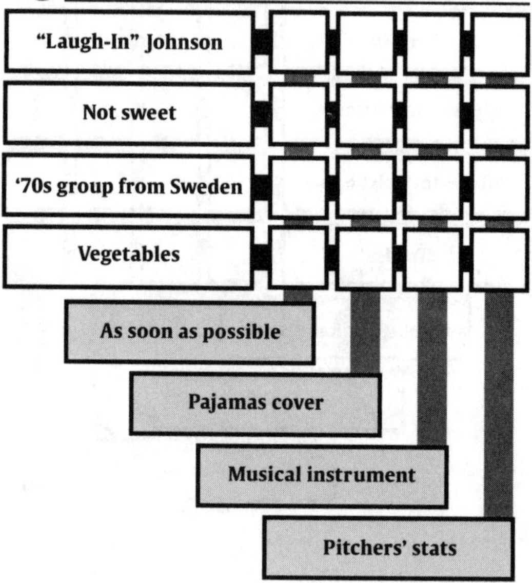

QuickCross™
"Laugh-In" Johnson
Not sweet
'70s group from Sweden
Vegetables
As soon as possible
Pajamas cover
Musical instrument
Pitchers' stats

USA TODAY

145

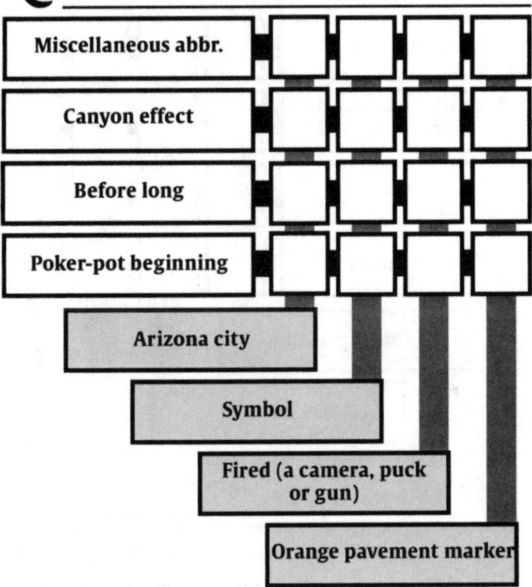
QuickCross™
Miscellaneous abbr.
Canyon effect
Before long
Poker-pot beginning
Arizona city
Symbol
Fired (a camera, puck or gun)
Orange pavement marker

USA TODAY

146

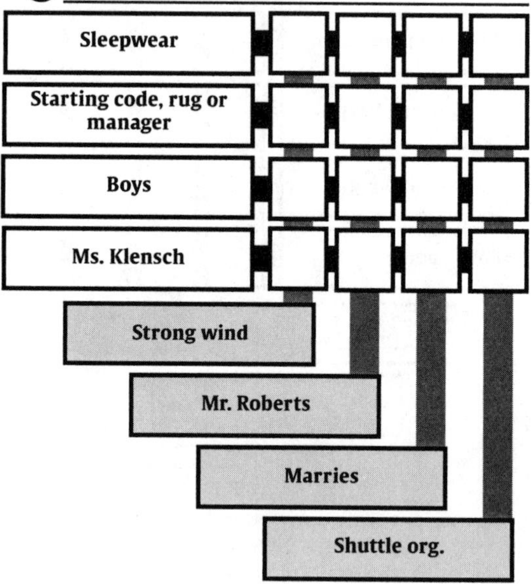
QuickCross™
Sleepwear
Starting code, rug or manager
Boys
Ms. Klensch
Strong wind
Mr. Roberts
Marries
Shuttle org.

USA TODAY®

147

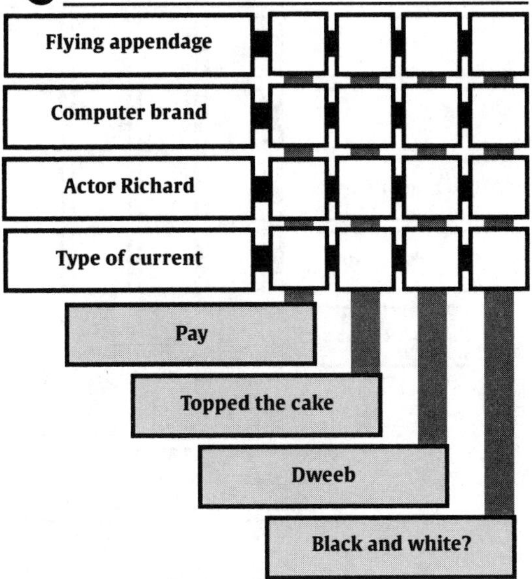
QuickCross™
Flying appendage
Computer brand
Actor Richard
Type of current
Pay
Topped the cake
Dweeb
Black and white?

USA TODAY

148

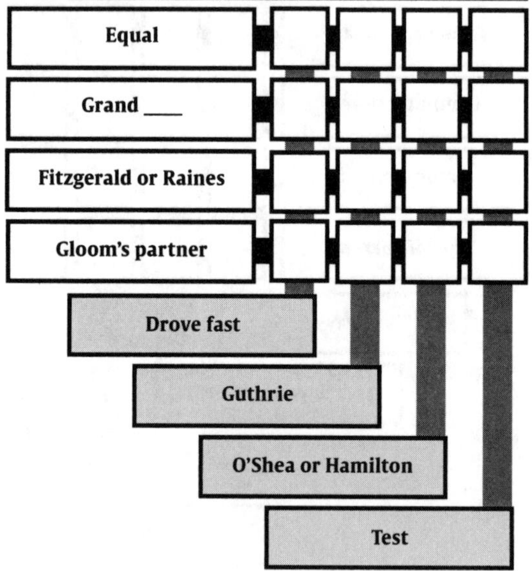
QuickCross™
Equal
Grand ___
Fitzgerald or Raines
Gloom's partner
Drove fast
Guthrie
O'Shea or Hamilton
Test

USA TODAY

149

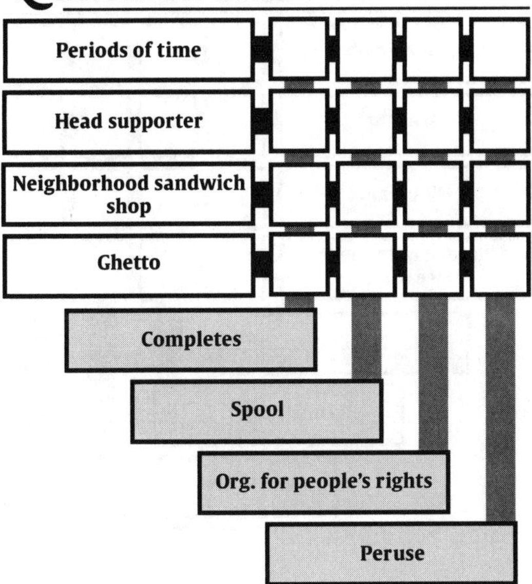
QuickCross™
Periods of time
Head supporter
Neighborhood sandwich shop
Ghetto
Completes
Spool
Org. for people's rights
Peruse

USA TODAY

150

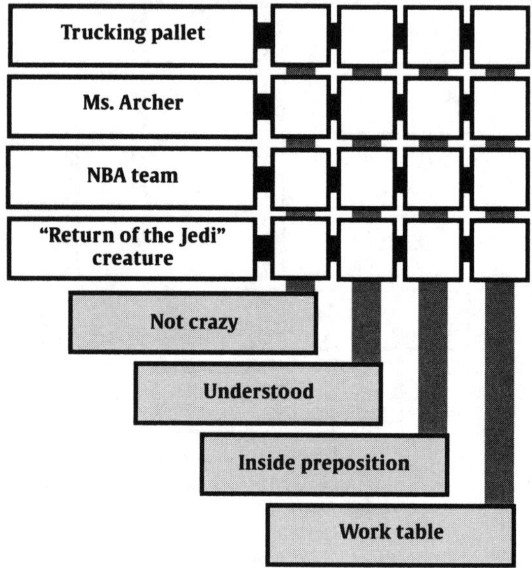
QuickCross™
Trucking pallet
Ms. Archer
NBA team
"Return of the Jedi" creature
Not crazy
Understood
Inside preposition
Work table

USA TODAY

QuickCross™

Across				
Fed. Emer. Mgt. Agency				
Neighborhood marketer				
Patty ___				
Football positions				

Down:

- Irene Cara title tune
- Some get mad, others get ...
- Forming cast
- Princesses Bala and Atta

152

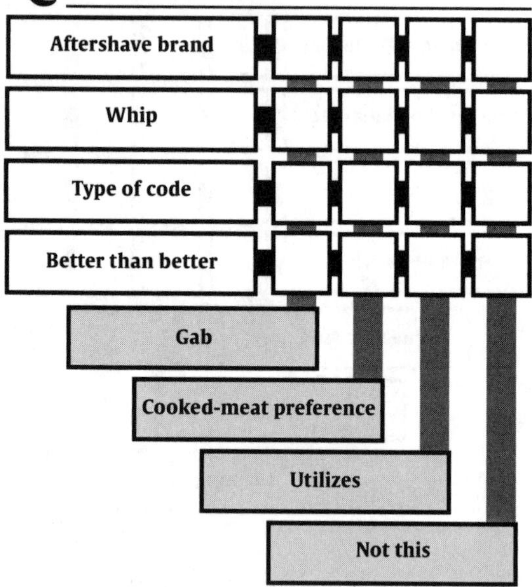
QuickCross™
Aftershave brand
Whip
Type of code
Better than better
Gab
Cooked-meat preference
Utilizes
Not this

153

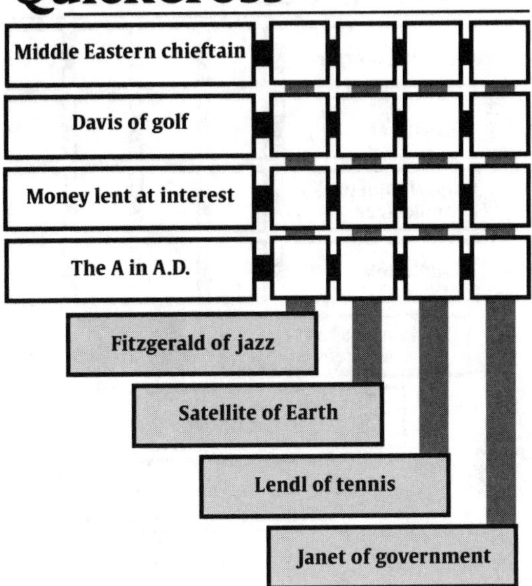
QuickCross™
Middle Eastern chieftain
Davis of golf
Money lent at interest
The A in A.D.
Fitzgerald of jazz
Satellite of Earth
Lendl of tennis
Janet of government

USA TODAY.

154

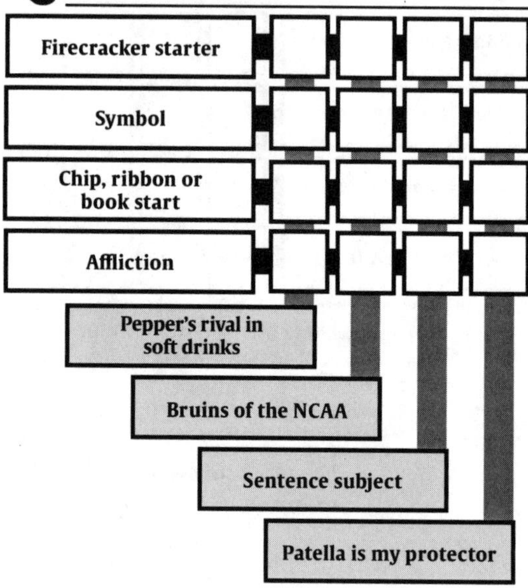
QuickCross™
Firecracker starter
Symbol
Chip, ribbon or book start
Affliction
Pepper's rival in soft drinks
Bruins of the NCAA
Sentence subject
Patella is my protector

USA TODAY

155

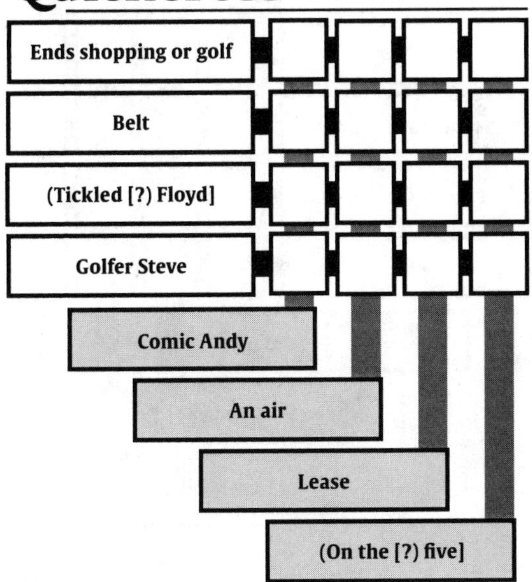
QuickCross™
Ends shopping or golf
Belt
(Tickled [?) Floyd]
Golfer Steve
Comic Andy
An air
Lease
(On the [?) five]

USA TODAY

156

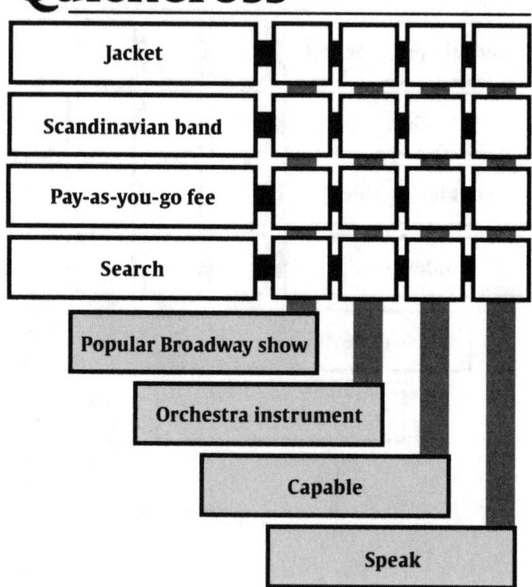
QuickCross™
Jacket
Scandinavian band
Pay-as-you-go fee
Search
Popular Broadway show
Orchestra instrument
Capable
Speak

USA TODAY

157

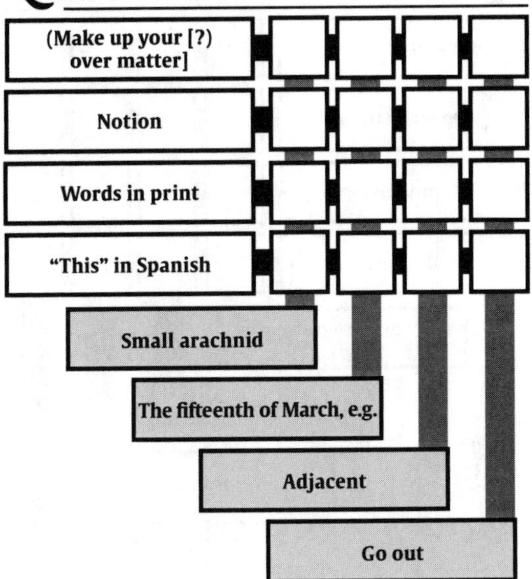
QuickCross™
(Make up your [?] over matter]
Notion
Words in print
"This" in Spanish
Small arachnid
The fifteenth of March, e.g.
Adjacent
Go out

USA TODAY

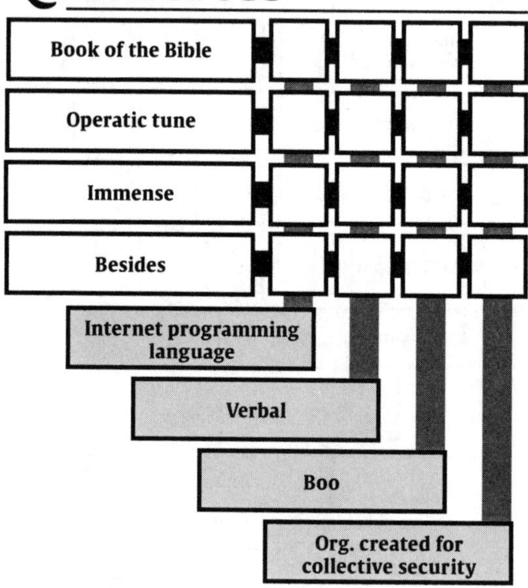
QuickCross™
Book of the Bible
Operatic tune
Immense
Besides
Internet programming language
Verbal
Boo
Org. created for collective security

USA TODAY

159

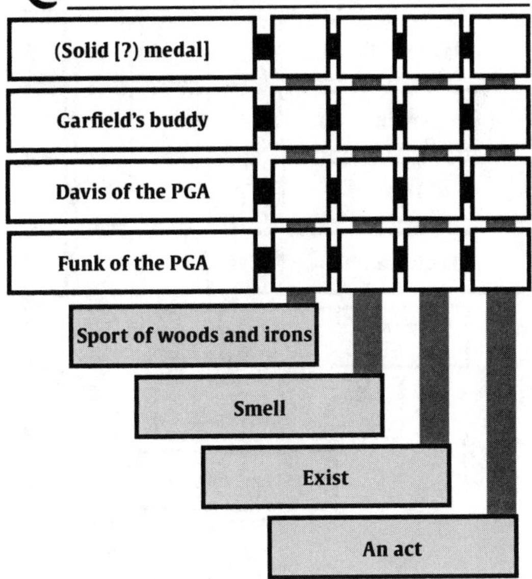
QuickCross™
(Solid [?) medal]
Garfield's buddy
Davis of the PGA
Funk of the PGA
Sport of woods and irons
Smell
Exist
An act

USA TODAY

160

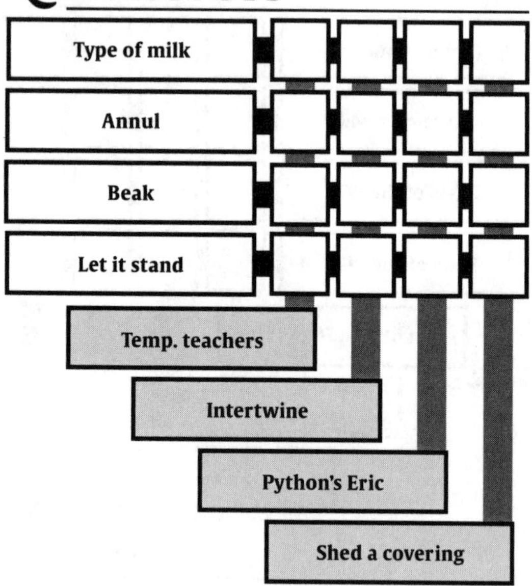
QuickCross™
Type of milk
Annul
Beak
Let it stand
Temp. teachers
Intertwine
Python's Eric
Shed a covering

161

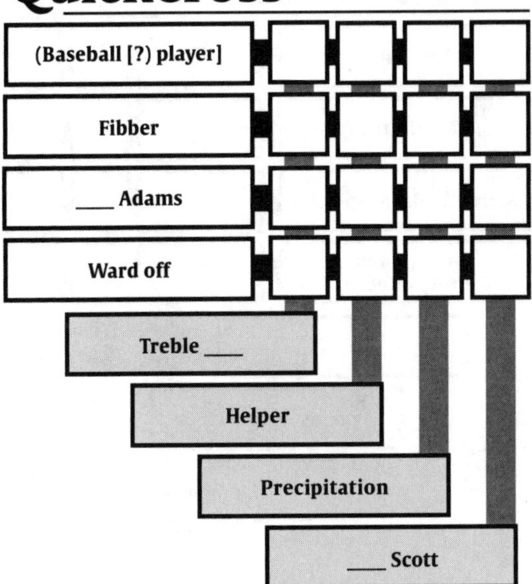
QuickCross™
(Baseball [?) player]
Fibber
____ Adams
Ward off
Treble ____
Helper
Precipitation
____ Scott

USA TODAY.

162

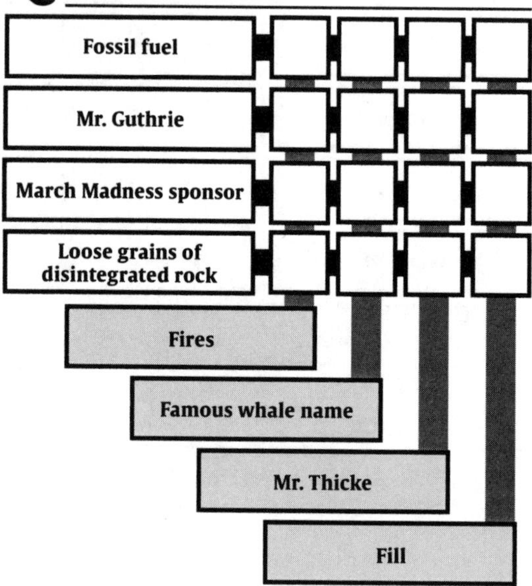
QuickCross™
Fossil fuel
Mr. Guthrie
March Madness sponsor
Loose grains of disintegrated rock
Fires
Famous whale name
Mr. Thicke
Fill

USA TODAY

QuickCross™

Waterfowl

Shaft

Region

Wording

Argument

Sported

Mr. Karras

Cool

164

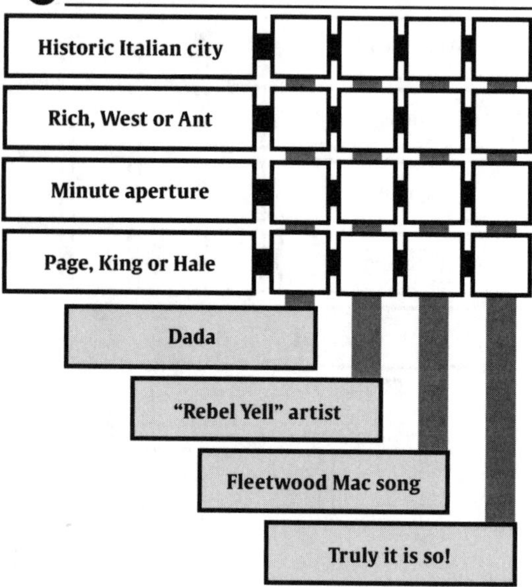

QuickCross™
Historic Italian city
Rich, West or Ant
Minute aperture
Page, King or Hale
Dada
"Rebel Yell" artist
Fleetwood Mac song
Truly it is so!

USA TODAY

165

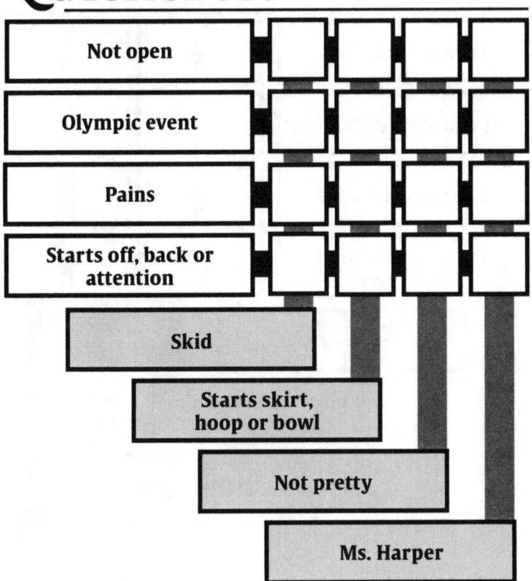
QuickCross™
Not open
Olympic event
Pains
Starts off, back or attention
Skid
Starts skirt, hoop or bowl
Not pretty
Ms. Harper

USA TODAY

166

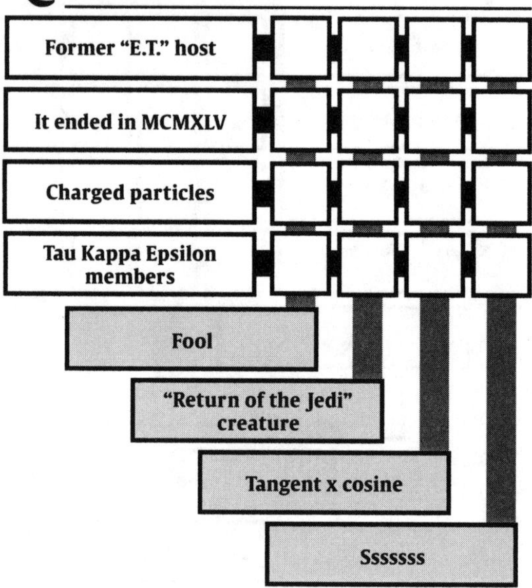
QuickCross™
Former "E.T." host
It ended in MCMXLV
Charged particles
Tau Kappa Epsilon members
Fool
"Return of the Jedi" creature
Tangent x cosine
Ssssss

USA TODAY

167

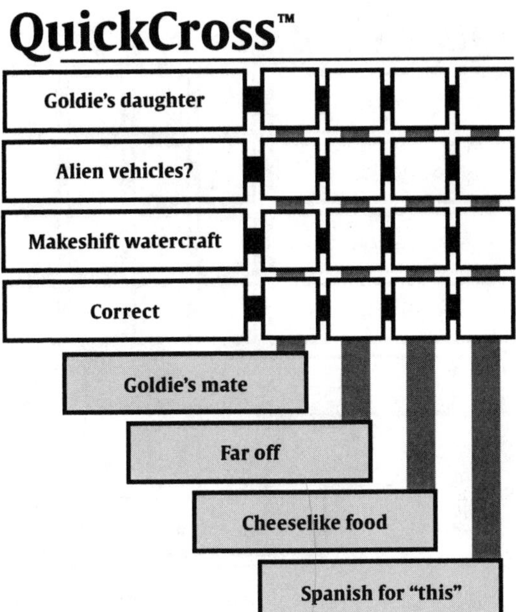
QuickCross™
Goldie's daughter
Alien vehicles?
Makeshift watercraft
Correct
Goldie's mate
Far off
Cheeselike food
Spanish for "this"

USA TODAY

168

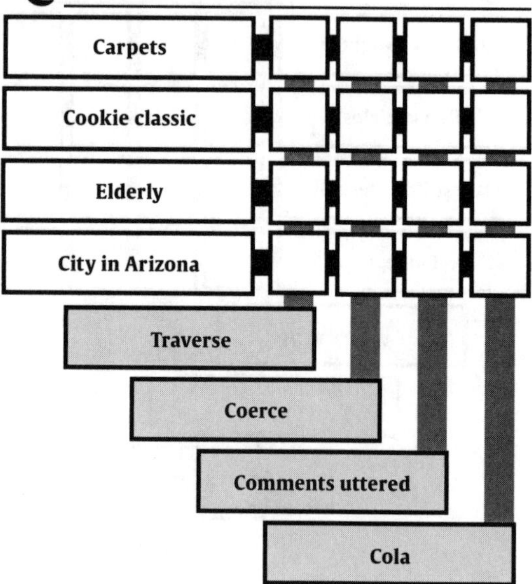
QuickCross™
Carpets
Cookie classic
Elderly
City in Arizona
Traverse
Coerce
Comments uttered
Cola

USA TODAY®

169

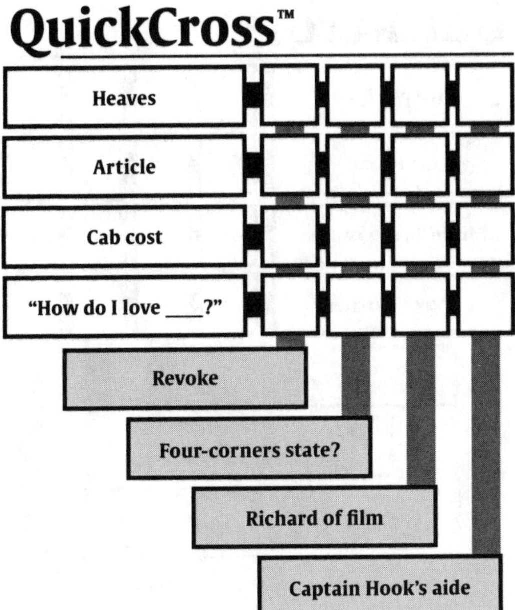
QuickCross™
Heaves
Article
Cab cost
"How do I love ____?"
Revoke
Four-corners state?
Richard of film
Captain Hook's aide

USA TODAY®

170

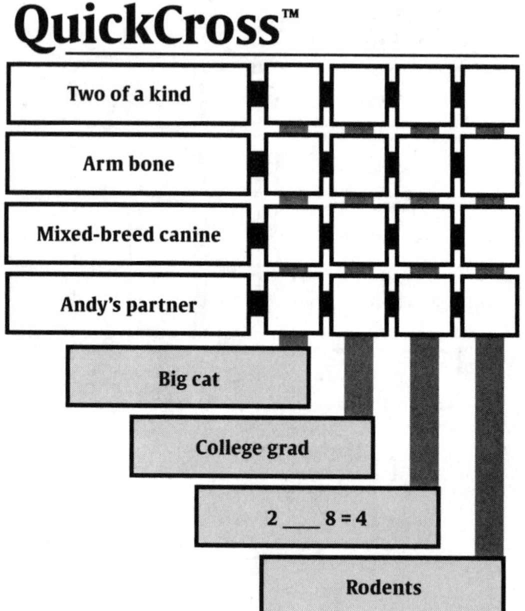
QuickCross™
Two of a kind
Arm bone
Mixed-breed canine
Andy's partner
Big cat
College grad
2 ___ 8 = 4
Rodents

USA TODAY

171

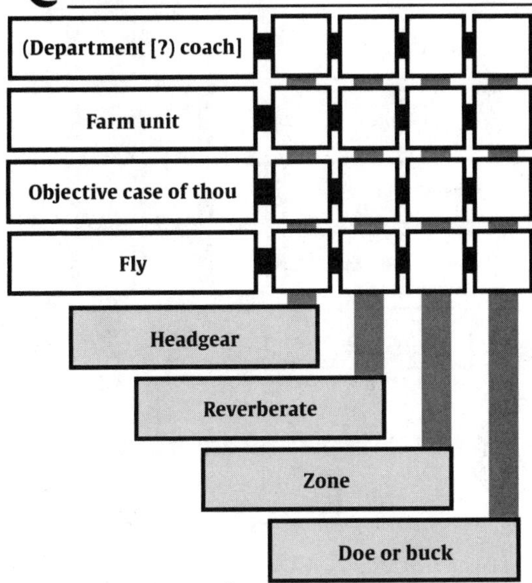
QuickCross™
(Department [?] coach]
Farm unit
Objective case of thou
Fly
Headgear
Reverberate
Zone
Doe or buck

USA TODAY

172

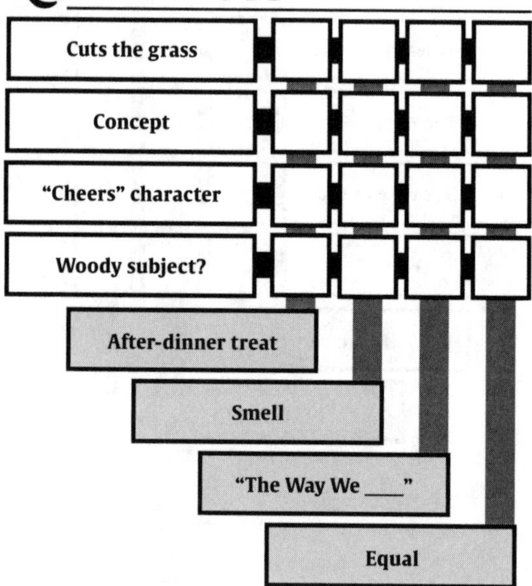
QuickCross™
Cuts the grass
Concept
"Cheers" character
Woody subject?
After-dinner treat
Smell
"The Way We ___"
Equal

QuickCross™

Robbers' nemeses

Telephone code

Actor Gregory

Do it, or ____!

Vampire garment

Mr. Hershiser

Muscles developed in a gym

Welfare

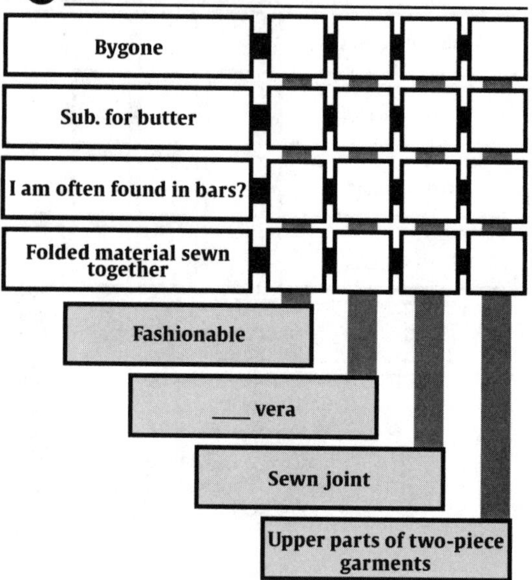
QuickCross™
Bygone
Sub. for butter
I am often found in bars?
Folded material sewn together
Fashionable
___ vera
Sewn joint
Upper parts of two-piece garments

USA TODAY

175

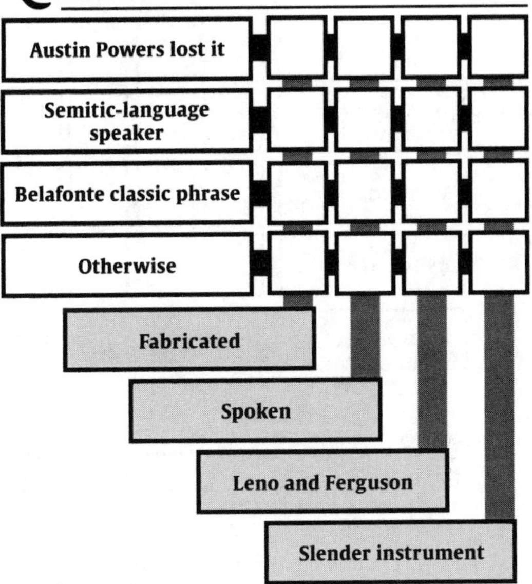
QuickCross™
Austin Powers lost it
Semitic-language speaker
Belafonte classic phrase
Otherwise
Fabricated
Spoken
Leno and Ferguson
Slender instrument

USA TODAY

176

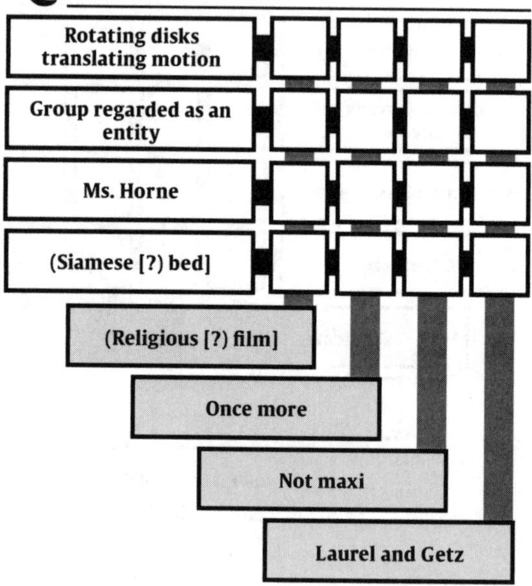
QuickCross™
Rotating disks translating motion
Group regarded as an entity
Ms. Horne
(Siamese [?) bed]
(Religious [?) film]
Once more
Not maxi
Laurel and Getz

QuickCross™

Clue				
Blot				
Reds and Browns are home here				
Sediment				
In addition				

Slammin' baseball player

Collins or Silvers

Greases

Dorothy's canine

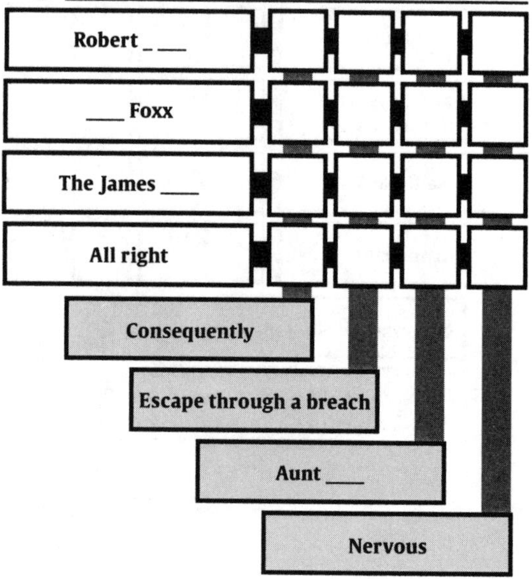
QuickCross™
Robert _ ___
___ Foxx
The James ___
All right
Consequently
Escape through a breach
Aunt ___
Nervous

USA TODAY

179

QuickCross™

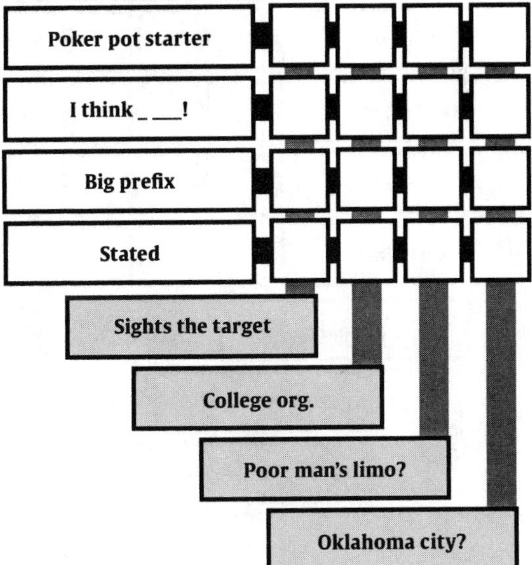

180

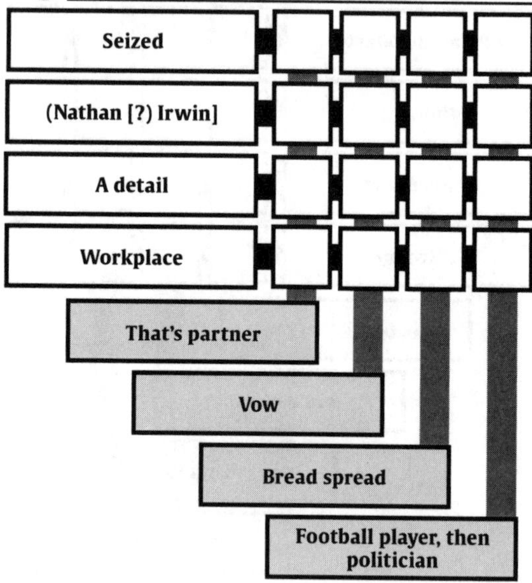
QuickCross™
Seized
(Nathan [?] Irwin]
A detail
Workplace
That's partner
Vow
Bread spread
Football player, then politician

QuickCross™

Plug in the plumbing				
Possess				
Positioned above				
Decline				

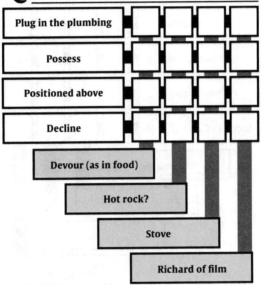

Devour (as in food)

Hot rock?

Stove

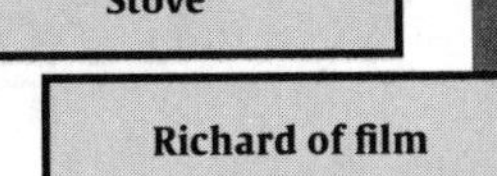

Richard of film

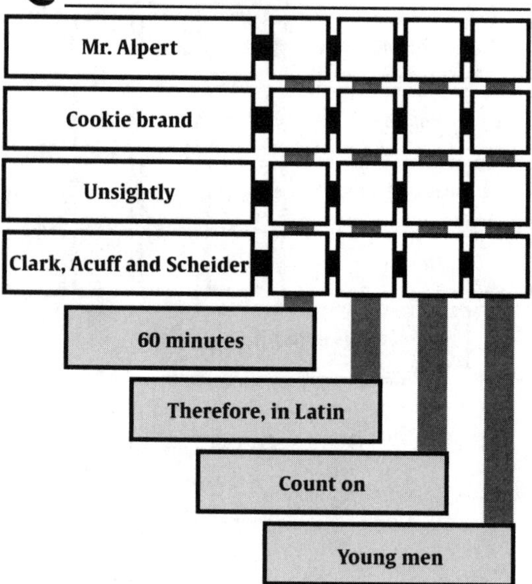
QuickCross™
Mr. Alpert
Cookie brand
Unsightly
Clark, Acuff and Scheider
60 minutes
Therefore, in Latin
Count on
Young men

USA TODAY

183

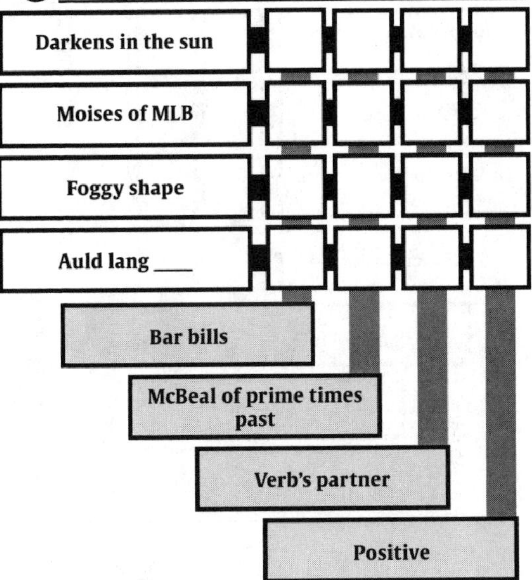

QuickCross™
Darkens in the sun
Moises of MLB
Foggy shape
Auld lang ____
Bar bills
McBeal of prime times past
Verb's partner
Positive

USA TODAY

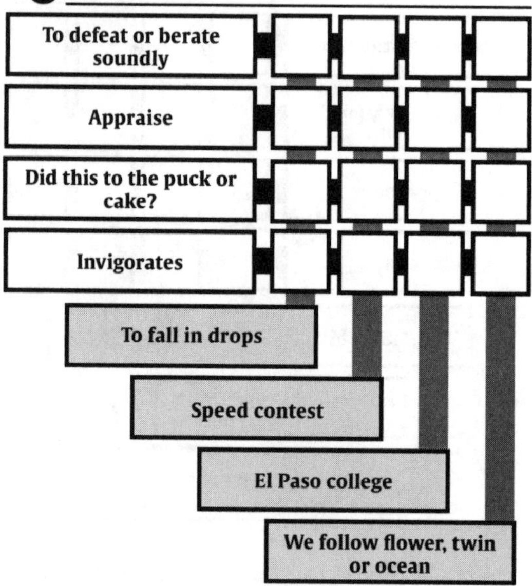
QuickCross™
To defeat or berate soundly
Appraise
Did this to the puck or cake?
Invigorates
To fall in drops
Speed contest
El Paso college
We follow flower, twin or ocean

USA TODAY®

185

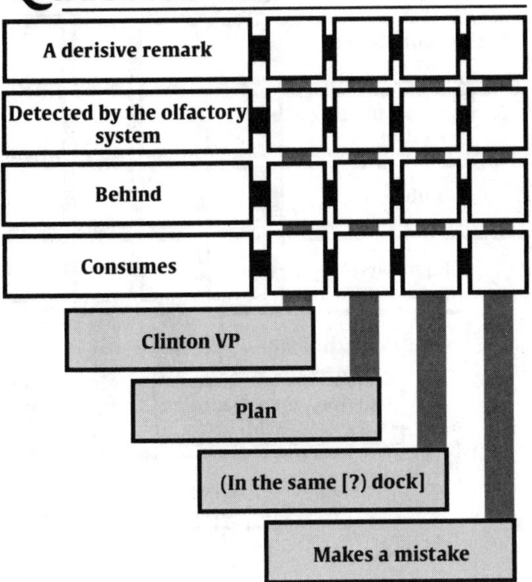
QuickCross™
A derisive remark
Detected by the olfactory system
Behind
Consumes
Clinton VP
Plan
(In the same [?] dock]
Makes a mistake

USA TODAY

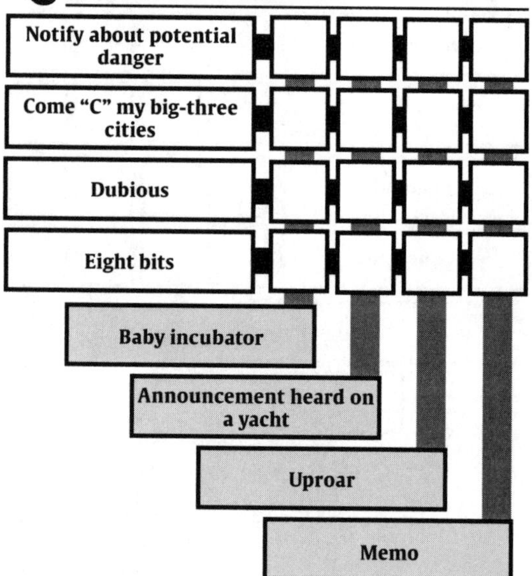
QuickCross™
Notify about potential danger
Come "C" my big-three cities
Dubious
Eight bits
Baby incubator
Announcement heard on a yacht
Uproar
Memo

USA TODAY®

187

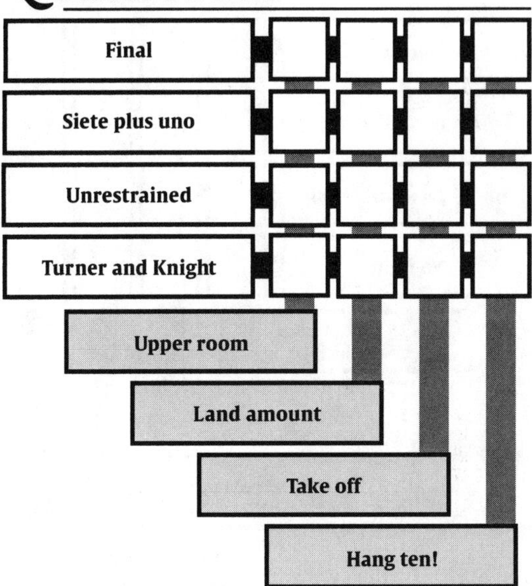
QuickCross™
Final
Siete plus uno
Unrestrained
Turner and Knight
Upper room
Land amount
Take off
Hang ten!

USA TODAY

188

QuickCross™

Decline

Two-way-radio closing

Son of Jacob and Leah

No cost!

(Cry [?) in sheep's clothing]

Affirm positively

Actress Campbell

North American lake

QuickCross™

- 160 square rods
- ____ carpet
- Alan, Stephen or Larry
- Sinks
- Questions
- ____ Pet
- Called
- Dozen items

190

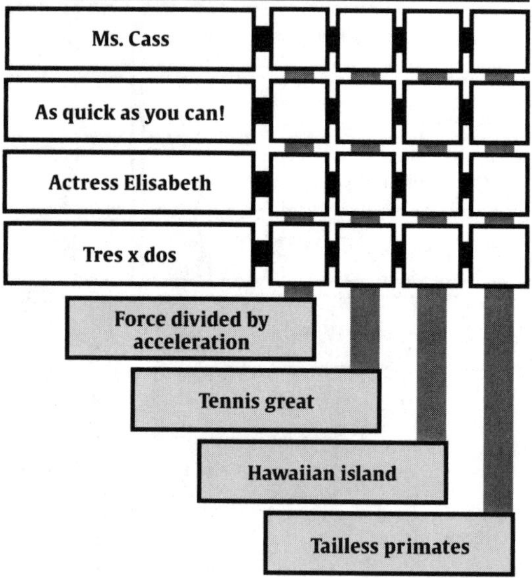
QuickCross™
Ms. Cass
As quick as you can!
Actress Elisabeth
Tres x dos
Force divided by acceleration
Tennis great
Hawaiian island
Tailless primates

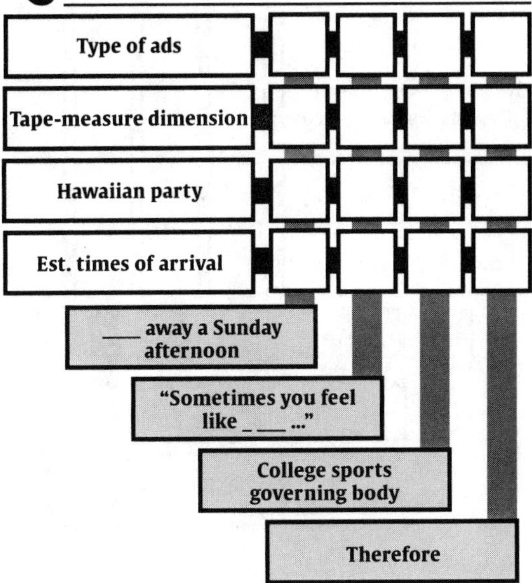
QuickCross™
Type of ads
Tape-measure dimension
Hawaiian party
Est. times of arrival
____ away a Sunday afternoon
"Sometimes you feel like _ ___..."
College sports governing body
Therefore

USA TODAY®

192

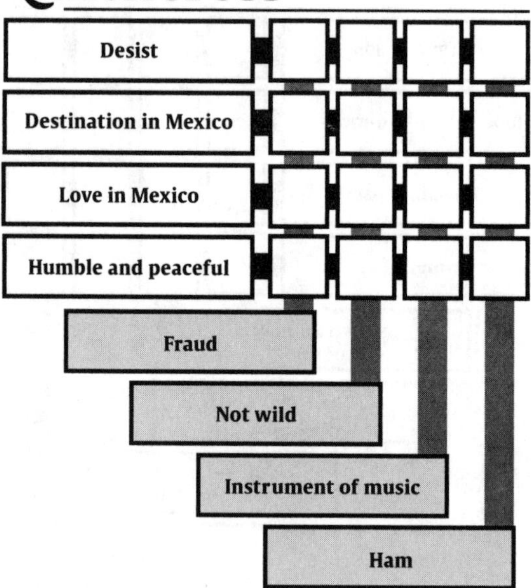
QuickCross™
Desist
Destination in Mexico
Love in Mexico
Humble and peaceful
Fraud
Not wild
Instrument of music
Ham

USA TODAY.

193

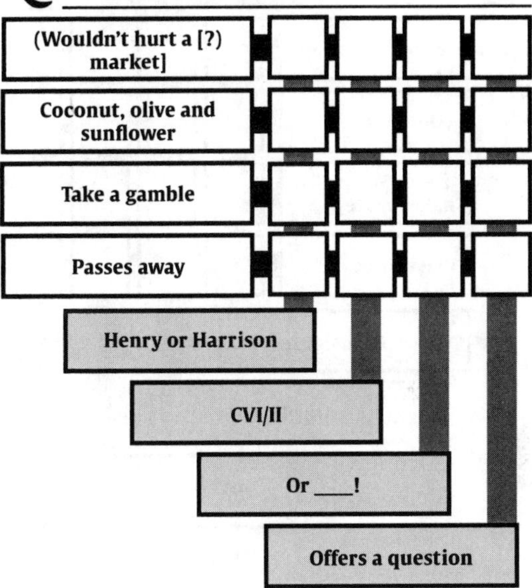
QuickCross™
(Wouldn't hurt a [?) market]
Coconut, olive and sunflower
Take a gamble
Passes away
Henry or Harrison
CVI/II
Or ___!
Offers a question

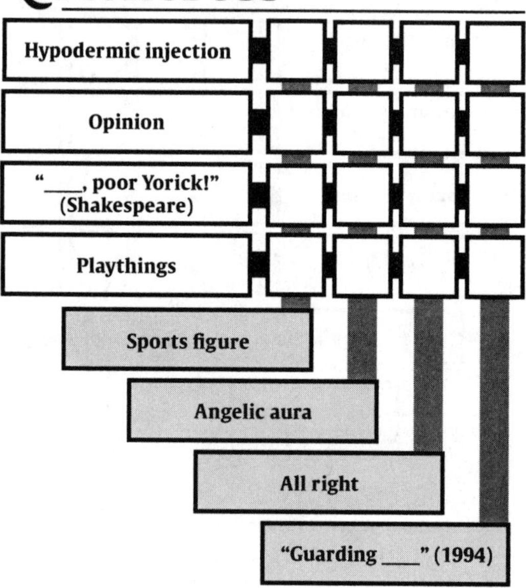
QuickCross™
Hypodermic injection
Opinion
"____, poor Yorick!" (Shakespeare)
Playthings
Sports figure
Angelic aura
All right
"Guarding ____" (1994)

USA TODAY

195

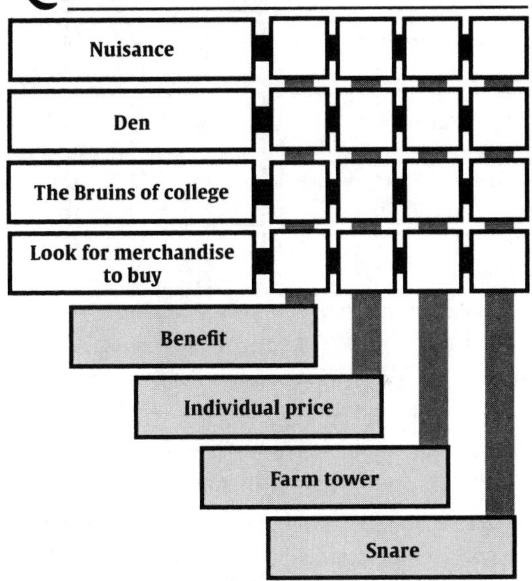
QuickCross™
Nuisance
Den
The Bruins of college
Look for merchandise to buy
Benefit
Individual price
Farm tower
Snare

USA TODAY.

196

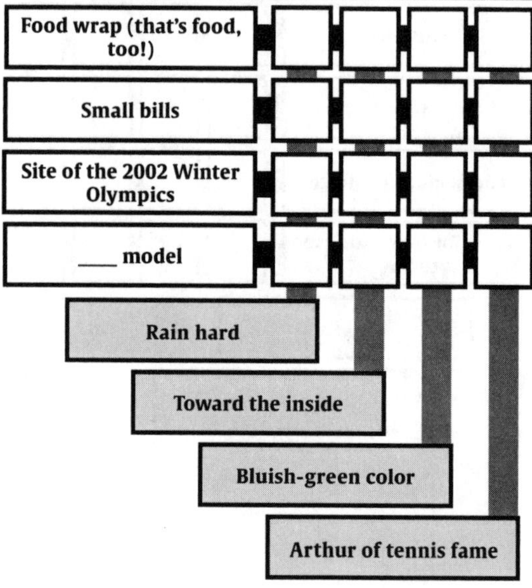
QuickCross™
Food wrap (that's food, too!)
Small bills
Site of the 2002 Winter Olympics
____ model
Rain hard
Toward the inside
Bluish-green color
Arthur of tennis fame

USA TODAY

QuickCross™

Bottle stopper

Kitchen appliance

Decrease

____ gin

Farm animals

____ Office

Janet ____

Leg joint

198

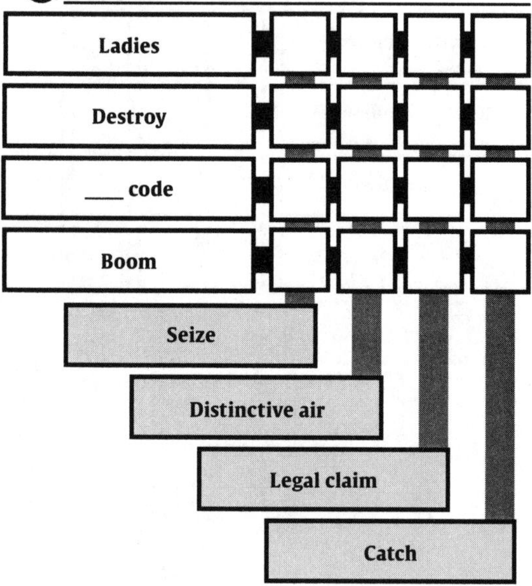
QuickCross™
Ladies
Destroy
___ code
Boom
Seize
Distinctive air
Legal claim
Catch

USA TODAY

QuickCross™

Clue				
(Play [?] of twine]				
China's continent				
St. Louis team				
Place				

Taverns

As fast as you can!

Hotel transportation?

(Dead [?] call]

200

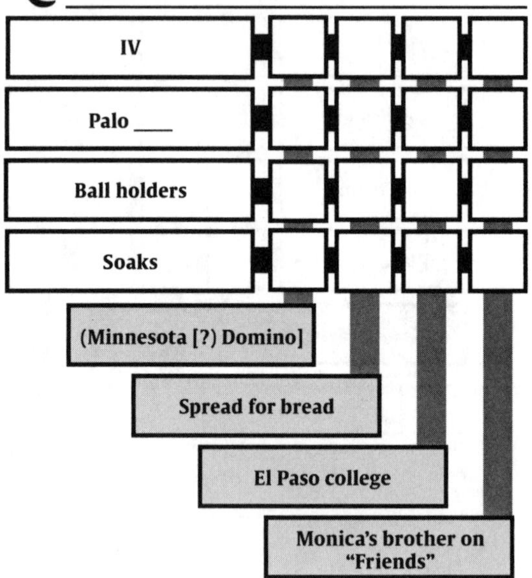
QuickCross™
IV
Palo ____
Ball holders
Soaks
(Minnesota [?] Domino]
Spread for bread
El Paso college
Monica's brother on "Friends"

USA TODAY

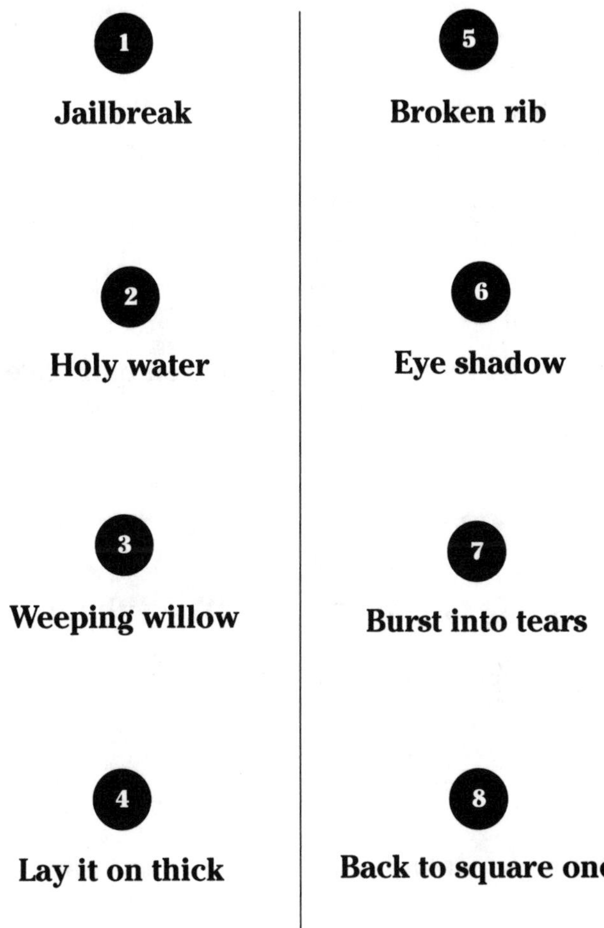
1
Jailbreak
2
Holy water
3
Weeping willow
4
Lay it on thick
5
Broken rib
6
Eye shadow
7
Burst into tears
8
Back to square one

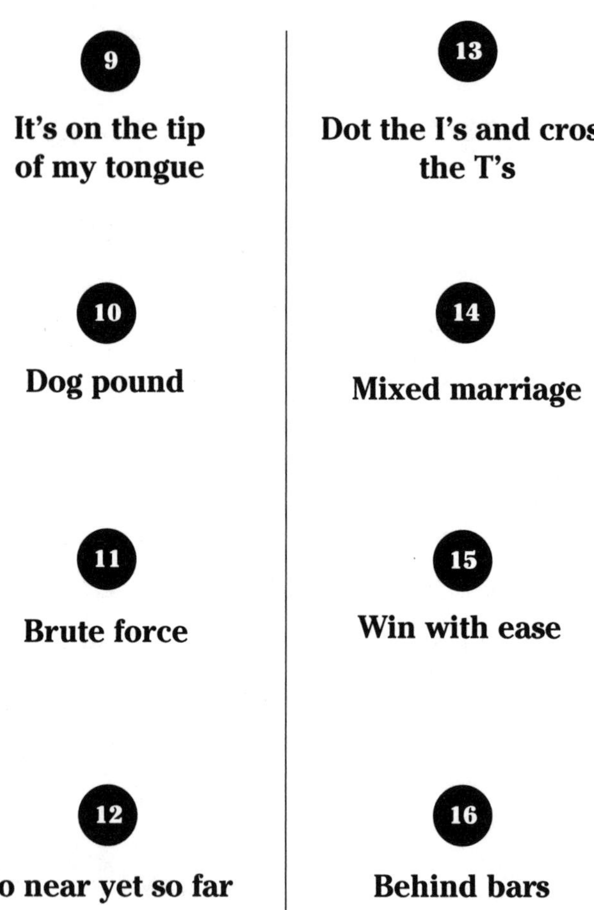
9
It's on the tip of my tongue
10
Dog pound
11
Brute force
12
So near yet so far
13
Dot the I's and cross the T's
14
Mixed marriage
15
Win with ease
16
Behind bars

17
Flash in the pan
18
You are out of your mind
19
Three blind mice
20
Read between the lines
21
All over the place
22
A lot to answer for
23
Tally Ho!
24
Crazy about you

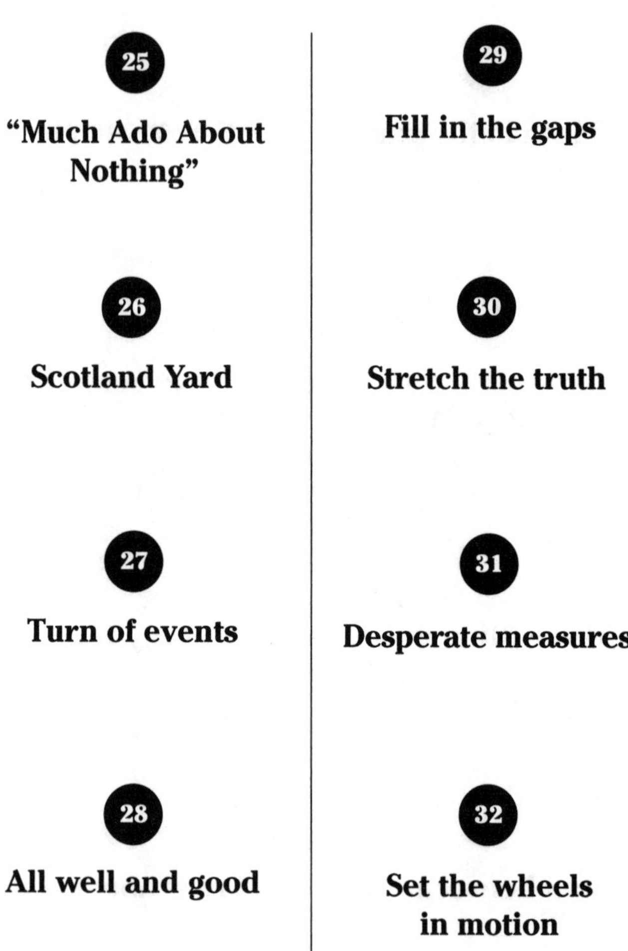
25
"Much Ado About Nothing"
26
Scotland Yard
27
Turn of events
28
All well and good
29
Fill in the gaps
30
Stretch the truth
31
Desperate measures
32
Set the wheels in motion

33

Cut the mustard

34

Razor sharp

35

Lie in wait

36

Hang-gliding

37

The devil is in the details

38

Crystal ball

39

Odd one out

40

The war between the sexes

41

I before E, except after C

42

Move up in the world

43

Both feet on the ground

44

A Tale of Two Cities

45

The last round-up

46

A borderline case

47

Lay money on it

48

Waste not, want not

49

First aid box

50

Through thick and thin

51

1	CATCH	COLD
2	COLD	WINTER
3	WINTER	STORM
4	STORM	WARNING
5	WARNING	TRACK
6	TRACK	STAR
7	STAR	WARS

53

1	MENTAL	HEALTH
2	HEALTH	CLUB
3	CLUB	SODA
4	SODA	POP
5	POP	FLY
6	FLY	FISHING
7	FISHING	LICENSE

52

1	BLACK	BOX
2	BOX	OFFICE
3	OFFICE	SPACE
4	SPACE	STATION
5	STATION	BREAK
6	BREAK	EVEN
7	EVEN	PAR

54

1	NEXT	SPRING
2	SPRING	WEDDING
3	WEDDING	DAY
4	DAY	JOB
5	JOB	ACTION
6	ACTION	MOVIE
7	MOVIE	CRITIC

55

1 NATIONAL TREASURE
2 TREASURE CHEST
3 CHEST OF
4 OF TIME
5 TIME WARNER
6 WARNER BROTHERS
7 BROTHERS GRIMM

56

1 SULFURIC ACID
2 ACID RAIN
3 RAIN FOREST
4 FOREST FIRE
5 FIRE ALARM
6 ALARM CLOCK
7 CLOCK RADIO

57

1 WONDER WHY
2 WHY NOT
3 NOT RIGHT
4 RIGHT TURN
5 TURN IN
6 IN THE
7 THE LINE

58

1 HEAVY TRAFFIC
2 TRAFFIC LIGHT
3 LIGHT SNOW
4 SNOW DAY
5 DAY OFF
6 OFF SWITCH
7 SWITCH PLACES

59

1 SEE RED
2 RED HOT
3 HOT COFFEE
4 COFFEE TABLE
5 TABLE SALT
6 SALT WATER
7 WATER WINGS

60

1 NOT FUNNY
2 FUNNY BONE
3 BONE DRY
4 DRY RUN
5 RUN OUT
6 OUT LOUD
7 LOUD SOUND

61

1 THE — MIDDLE
2 MIDDLE — GROUND
3 GROUND — CHUCK
4 CHUCK — WAGON
5 WAGON — TRAIN
6 TRAIN — STATION
7 STATION — HOUSE

62

1 NOT — TRUE
2 TRUE — BLUE
3 BLUE — SKY
4 SKY — HIGH
5 HIGH — TEA
6 TEA — BAG
7 BAG — BOY

63

1 GROW — OLD
2 OLD — HOUSE
3 HOUSE — KEY
4 KEY — CHAIN
5 CHAIN — LETTER
6 LETTER — CARRIER
7 CARRIER — PIGEON

64

1 VENOMOUS — SPIDER
2 SPIDER — MONKEY
3 MONKEY — BUSINESS
4 BUSINESS — PLAN
5 PLAN — OF
6 OF — THE
7 THE — DOORS

65

1 COURT — MARTIAL
2 MARTIAL — LAW
3 LAW — SCHOOL
4 SCHOOL — DISTRICT
5 DISTRICT — ATTORNEY
6 ATTORNEY — GENERAL
7 GENERAL — MILLS

66

1 AT — FIRST
2 FIRST — BLOOD
3 BLOOD — CELL
4 CELL — PHONE
5 PHONE — BOOK
6 BOOK — CLUB
7 CLUB — CAR

67

1	SNOW	WHITE
2	WHITE	HOUSE
3	HOUSE	TRAILER
4	TRAILER	PARK
5	PARK	SERVICE
6	SERVICE	CHARGE
7	CHARGE	AHEAD

68

1	AT	LAST
2	LAST	CALL
3	CALL	OFF
4	OFF	GUARD
5	GUARD	POST
6	POST	OFFICE
7	OFFICE	SUPPLIES

69

1	PRIVATE	PROPERTY
2	PROPERTY	TAX
3	TAX	BASE
4	BASE	HIT
5	HIT	PARADE
6	PARADE	ROUTE
7	ROUTE	NUMBER

70

1	SUDDEN	DEATH
2	DEATH	PENALTY
3	PENALTY	KICK
4	KICK	BOXING
5	BOXING	MATCH
6	MATCH	POINT
7	POINT	OUT

71

1	DAILY	DOUBLE
2	DOUBLE	PLAY
3	PLAY	TIME
4	TIME	OFF
5	OFF	COLOR
6	COLOR	TV
7	TV	PROGRAM

72

1	FRANKFORT	KENTUCKY
2	KENTUCKY	FRIED
3	FRIED	CLAM
4	CLAM	SHELL
5	SHELL	OIL
6	OIL	CAN
7	CAN	OPENER

73

1 EXTRA — LARGE
2 LARGE — FAMILY
3 FAMILY — TREE
4 TREE — BRANCH
5 BRANCH — OUT
6 OUT — LOUD
7 LOUD — MOUTH

74

1 TURNING — POINT
2 POINT — OF
3 OF — TIME
4 TIME — MAGAZINE
5 MAGAZINE — STAND
6 STAND — BY
7 BY — THE

75

1 FRESH — AIR
2 AIR — BUBBLE
3 BUBBLE — GUM
4 GUM — LINE
5 LINE — UP
6 UP — NORTH
7 NORTH — POLE

76

1 MEXICAN — BORDER
2 BORDER — GUARD
3 GUARD — DUTY
4 DUTY — FREE
5 FREE — GIFT
6 GIFT — WRAP
7 WRAP — UP

77

1 TOM — THUMB
2 THUMB — PRINT
3 PRINT — SCREEN
4 SCREEN — NAME
5 NAME — PLATE
6 PLATE — GLASS
7 GLASS — EYE

78

1 BAKING — SODA
2 SODA — POP
3 POP — MUSIC
4 MUSIC — VIDEO
5 VIDEO — RENTAL
6 RENTAL — CAR
7 CAR — DEALER

79

1 CHEMICAL REACTION
2 REACTION ⤢ TIME
3 TIME ⤢ TRIAL
4 TRIAL ⤢ AND
5 AND ⤢ HOW
6 HOW ⤢ DOES
7 DOES ⤢ IT

80

1 FIREWORKS DISPLAY
2 DISPLAY ⤢ CASE
3 CASE ⤢ IN
4 IN ⤢ TOO
5 TOO ⤢ BAD
6 BAD ⤢ COLD
7 COLD ⤢ CALL

81

1 BEAT THE
2 THE ⤢ DEEP
3 DEEP ⤢ SOUTH
4 SOUTH ⤢ VIETNAM
5 VIETNAM ⤢ WAR
6 WAR ⤢ CRIME
7 CRIME ⤢ BOSS

82

1 GOOD TIMES
2 TIMES ⤢ SQUARE
3 SQUARE ⤢ OFF
4 OFF ⤢ DEAD
5 DEAD ⤢ MAN
6 MAN ⤢ GROUP
7 GROUP ⤢ EFFORT

83

1 NOT EASY
2 EASY ⤢ MONEY
3 MONEY ⤢ CLIP
4 CLIP ⤢ ON
5 ON ⤢ BOARD
6 BOARD ⤢ OF
7 OF ⤢ FACT

84

1 DRAG RACE
2 RACE ⤢ CAR
3 CAR ⤢ CARE
4 CARE ⤢ FOR
5 FOR ⤢ DINNER
6 DINNER ⤢ TABLE
7 TABLE ⤢ MANNERS

85

1 DEEP — WATER
2 WATER ⤢ GUN
3 GUN ⤢ CHAMBER
4 CHAMBER ⤢ MUSIC
5 MUSIC ⤢ BOX
6 BOX ⤢ UP
7 UP ⤢ TO

86

1 LOOK — AT
2 AT ⤢ LARGE
3 LARGE ⤢ DOG
4 DOG ⤢ HOUSE
5 HOUSE ⤢ GUEST
6 GUEST ⤢ STAR
7 STAR ⤢ WARS

87

1 PRIME — NUMBER
2 NUMBER ⤢ TWO
3 TWO ⤢ GRAND
4 GRAND ⤢ SLAM
5 SLAM ⤢ DUNK
6 DUNK ⤢ SHOT
7 SHOT ⤢ PUT

88

1 TABLE — SALT
2 SALT ⤢ WATER
3 WATER ⤢ BUFFALO
4 BUFFALO ⤢ BILL
5 BILL ⤢ COSBY
6 COSBY ⤢ SHOW
7 SHOW ⤢ OFF

89

1 TERM — PAPER
2 PAPER ⤢ CHASE
3 CHASE ⤢ DOWN
4 DOWN ⤢ HOME
5 HOME ⤢ GAME
6 GAME ⤢ FACE
7 FACE ⤢ OFF

90

1 JACK — BLACK
2 BLACK ⤢ INK
3 INK ⤢ JET
4 JET ⤢ ENGINE
5 ENGINE ⤢ OIL
6 OIL ⤢ CAN
7 CAN ⤢ OPENER

91

1	TOO	BIG
2	BIG	SHOT
3	SHOT	GLASS
4	GLASS	EYE
5	EYE	DOCTOR
6	DOCTOR	WHO
7	WHO	CARES

92

1	ANOTHER	LOOK
2	LOOK	FIRST
3	FIRST	TAKE
4	TAKE	OVER
5	OVER	WITH
6	WITH	LOVE
7	LOVE	LETTER

93

1	JUNIOR	HIGH
2	HIGH	JUMP
3	JUMP	IN
4	IN	ONE
5	ONE	DAY
6	DAY	JOB
7	JOB	SEARCH

94

1	BIG	HEAD
2	HEAD	NORTH
3	NORTH	ATLANTIC
4	ATLANTIC	TIME
5	TIME	ZONE
6	ZONE	DEFENSE
7	DEFENSE	MECHANISM

95

1	HIGHWAY	PATROL
2	PATROL	CAR
3	CAR	POOL
4	POOL	WATER
5	WATER	BUFFALO
6	BUFFALO	BILL
7	BILL	GATES

96

1	NOT	FAR
2	FAR	EAST
3	EAST	COAST
4	COAST	GUARD
5	GUARD	DOG
6	DOG	COLLAR
7	COLLAR	BONE

97

1 PRIVATE — CLUB
2 CLUB — SODA
3 SODA — POP
4 POP — FLY
5 FLY — FISHING
6 FISHING — LINE
7 LINE — DANCING

98

1 LIVING — DEAD
2 DEAD — SEA
3 SEA — LION
4 LION — KING
5 KING — SNAKE
6 SNAKE — OIL
7 OIL — SLICK

99

1 DIE — HARD
2 HARD — DRIVE
3 DRIVE — IN
4 IN — STEP
5 STEP — DOWN
6 DOWN — PAYMENT
7 PAYMENT — PLAN

100

1 NOT — SO
2 SO — LONG
3 LONG — PASS
4 PASS — OUT
5 OUT — OF
6 OF — WAR
7 WAR — GAMES

101

1 BLUE — SKY
2 SKY — HIGH
3 HIGH — QUALITY
4 QUALITY — CONTROL
5 CONTROL — CENTER
6 CENTER — COURT
7 COURT — TV

102

1 GIVE — UP
2 UP — CLOSE
3 CLOSE — CALL
4 CALL — OFF
5 OFF — GUARD
6 GUARD — DOG
7 DOG — TAGS

103

1 ABSOLUTE — ZERO
2 ZERO — IN
3 IN — TIME
4 TIME — LINE
5 LINE — OF
6 OF — COURSE
7 COURSE — CHANGE

104

1 ALL — DONE
2 DONE — FOR
3 FOR — SALE
4 SALE — PRICE
5 PRICE — IS
6 IS — MONEY
7 MONEY — BAGS

105

1 VERY — BAD
2 BAD — DOG
3 DOG — BONE
4 BONE — DRY
5 DRY — OUT
6 OUT — TO
7 TO — GO

106

1 NOT — FAIR
2 FAIR — PRICE
3 PRICE — WAR
4 WAR — PAINT
5 PAINT — BY
6 BY — THE
7 THE — BEATLES

107

1 SPENDING — MONEY
2 MONEY — BACK
3 BACK — UP
4 UP — NORTH
5 NORTH — SEA
6 SEA — LION
7 LION — KING

108

1 TRY — HARD
2 HARD — ROCK
3 ROCK — MUSIC
4 MUSIC — BOX
5 BOX — KITE
6 KITE — STRING
7 STRING — OUT

109

1 NO — GOOD
2 GOOD — CATCH
3 CATCH — COLD
4 COLD — FRONT
5 FRONT — BUMPER
6 BUMPER — CAR
7 CAR — RACE

110

1 BIG — TOP
2 TOP — SECRET
3 SECRET — CODE
4 CODE — NAME
5 NAME — THAT
6 THAT — GIRL
7 GIRL — SCOUT

111

1 HELP — ME
2 ME — TOO
3 TOO — THIN
4 THIN — ICE
5 ICE — CREAM
6 CREAM — SODA
7 SODA — BOTTLE

112

1 NOT — SO
2 SO — LONG
3 LONG — DAY
4 DAY — GAME
5 GAME — SHOW
6 SHOW — OFF
7 OFF — BASE

113

1 VOICE — BOX
2 BOX — TURTLE
3 TURTLE — SOUP
4 SOUP — KITCHEN
5 KITCHEN — TABLE
6 TABLE — TENNIS
7 TENNIS — LESSON

114

1 SALVATION — ARMY
2 ARMY — BASE
3 BASE — PAY
4 PAY — RAISE
5 RAISE — UP
6 UP — CLOSE
7 CLOSE — CALL

115

1 STEPHEN — KING
2 KING ↙↗ SNAKE
3 SNAKE ↙↗ PIT
4 PIT ↙↗ STOP
5 STOP ↙↗ SIGN
6 SIGN ↙↗ LANGUAGE
7 LANGUAGE ↙↗ BARRIER

116

1 NOT — IN
2 IN ↙↗ STOCK
3 STOCK ↙↗ MARKET
4 MARKET ↙↗ PRICE
5 PRICE ↙↗ WAR
6 WAR ↙↗ ZONE
7 ZONE ↙↗ DEFENSE

117

1 WILD — ANIMAL
2 ANIMAL ↙↗ KINGDOM
3 KINGDOM ↙↗ COME
4 COME ↙↗ HOME
5 HOME ↙↗ PAY
6 PAY ↙↗ BACK
7 BACK ↙↗ AWAY

118

1 EXTRA — CREDIT
2 CREDIT ↙↗ CARD
3 CARD ↙↗ GAME
4 GAME ↙↗ POINT
5 POINT ↙↗ BREAK
6 BREAK ↙↗ OFF
7 OFF ↙↗ GUARD

119

1 CHRIS — ROCK
2 ROCK ↙↗ SALT
3 SALT ↙↗ LAKE
4 LAKE ↙↗ ONTARIO
5 ONTARIO ↙↗ CANADA
6 CANADA ↙↗ DRY
7 DRY ↙↗ WELL

120

1 BAD — DOG
2 DOG ↙↗ POUND
3 POUND ↙↗ STERLING
4 STERLING ↙↗ SILVER
5 SILVER ↙↗ SCREEN
6 SCREEN ↙↗ TEST
7 TEST ↙↗ SCORE

121

1	LIMITED	TIME
2	TIME	WARP
3	WARP	SPEED
4	SPEED	BUMP
5	BUMP	OFF
6	OFF	KEY
7	KEY	LIME

122

1	DR.	NO
2	NO	GOOD
3	GOOD	WILL
4	WILL	SMITH
5	SMITH	AND
6	AND	OUT
7	OUT	COLD

123

1	TOM	CRUISE
2	CRUISE	SHIP
3	SHIP	OUT
4	OUT	OF
5	OF	LIGHT
6	LIGHT	SHOW
7	SHOW	UP

124

1	EASTER	ISLAND
2	ISLAND	COUNTRY
3	COUNTRY	CLUB
4	CLUB	SODA
5	SODA	FOUNTAIN
6	FOUNTAIN	PEN
7	PEN	PAL

125

1	PRIVATE	PROPERTY
2	PROPERTY	TAX
3	TAX	CUT
4	CUT	BACK
5	BACK	OUT
6	OUT	LOUD
7	LOUD	MOUTH

126

H	A	T	S
A	L	A	I
R	O	L	L
P	E	C	K

127

S	O	L	D
A	R	E	A
N	E	A	R
D	O	N	E

128

C	A	R	E
O	B	E	Y
N	O	N	E
E	W	E	S

129

A	B	B	A
B	A	R	R
E	L	A	M
L	E	G	S

130

C	E	L	L
O	R	E	O
P	I	N	T
S	E	T	S

131

S	E	I	S
A	C	R	E
S	H	O	E
S	O	C	K

132

S A F E
O P E N
L I E D
D A D S

133

P A R K
A L O E
S T O P
S O F T

134

F O R M
I D E A
S O D S
T R O T

135

D R E W
R A R E
O V A L
P E S T

136

S A L T
E R I E
L A K E
A L E S

137

B E A T
U C L A
S H A M
H O N E

138

S	A	K	E
A	I	R	Y
G	L	U	E
A	S	K	S

139

J	I	B	S
I	D	O	L
G	O	R	E
S	T	E	W

140

S	S	T	S
A	L	O	E
N	O	T	E
G	W	E	N

141

J	O	H	N
E	R	I	E
T	A	K	E
S	L	E	D

142

R	S	V	P
A	W	O	L
N	A	T	O
K	N	E	W

143

G	A	I	N
O	B	O	E
U	L	N	A
T	E	S	T

144

A	R	T	E
S	O	U	R
A	B	B	A
P	E	A	S

145

M	I	S	C
E	C	H	O
S	O	O	N
A	N	T	E

146

G	O	W	N
A	R	E	A
L	A	D	S
E	L	S	A

147

W	I	N	G
A	C	E	R
G	E	R	E
E	D	D	Y

148

S	A	M	E
P	R	I	X
E	L	L	A
D	O	O	M

149

E	R	A	S
N	E	C	K
D	E	L	I
S	L	U	M

150

S	K	I	D
A	N	N	E
N	E	T	S
E	W	O	K

151

F	E	M	A
A	V	O	N
M	E	L	T
E	N	D	S

152

B	R	U	T
L	A	S	H
A	R	E	A
B	E	S	T

153

E	M	I	R
L	O	V	E
L	O	A	N
A	N	N	O

154

P	U	N	K
I	C	O	N
B	L	U	E
B	A	N	E

155

C	A	R	T
A	R	E	A
P	I	N	K
P	A	T	E

156

C	O	A	T
A	B	B	A
T	O	L	L
S	E	E	K

157

M	I	N	D
I	D	E	A
T	E	X	T
E	S	T	E

158

J	O	H	N
A	R	I	A
V	A	S	T
A	L	S	O

159

G	O	L	D
O	D	I	E
L	O	V	E
F	R	E	D

160

S	K	I	M
U	N	D	O
B	I	L	L
S	T	E	T

161

C	A	R	D
L	I	A	R
E	D	I	E
F	E	N	D

162

C	O	A	L
A	R	L	O
N	C	A	A
S	A	N	D

163

S	W	A	N
P	O	L	E
A	R	E	A
T	E	X	T

164

P	I	S	A
A	D	A	M
P	O	R	E
A	L	A	N

165

S	H	U	T
L	U	G	E
I	L	L	S
P	A	Y	S

166

T	E	S	H
W	W	I	I
I	O	N	S
T	K	E	S

167

K	A	T	E
U	F	O	S
R	A	F	T
T	R	U	E

168

R	U	G	S
O	R	E	O
A	G	E	D
M	E	S	A

169

L	U	G	S
I	T	E	M
F	A	R	E
T	H	E	E

170

P	A	I	R
U	L	N	A
M	U	T	T
A	M	O	S

171

H	E	A	D
A	C	R	E
T	H	E	E
S	O	A	R

172

M	O	W	S
I	D	E	A
N	O	R	M
T	R	E	E

173

C	O	P	S
A	R	E	A
P	E	C	K
E	L	S	E

174

P	A	S	T
O	L	E	O
S	O	A	P
H	E	M	S

175

M	O	J	O
A	R	A	B
D	A	Y	O
E	L	S	E

176

C	A	M	S
U	N	I	T
L	E	N	A
T	W	I	N

177

S	P	O	T
O	H	I	O
S	I	L	T
A	L	S	O

178

E	L	E	E
R	E	D	D
G	A	N	G
O	K	A	Y

179

A	N	T	E
I	C	A	N
M	A	X	I
S	A	I	D

180

T	O	O	K
H	A	L	E
I	T	E	M
S	H	O	P

181

C	L	O	G
H	A	V	E
O	V	E	R
W	A	N	E

182

H	E	R	B
O	R	E	O
U	G	L	Y
R	O	Y	S

183

T	A	N	S
A	L	O	U
B	L	U	R
S	Y	N	E

184

D	R	U	B
R	A	T	E
I	C	E	D
P	E	P	S

185

G	I	B	E
O	D	O	R
R	E	A	R
E	A	T	S

186

W	A	R	N
O	H	I	O
M	O	O	T
B	Y	T	E

187

L	A	S	T
O	C	H	O
F	R	E	E
T	E	D	S

188

W	A	N	E
O	V	E	R
L	E	V	I
F	R	E	E

189

A	C	R	E
S	H	A	G
K	I	N	G
S	A	G	S

190

M	A	M	A
A	S	A	P
S	H	U	E
S	E	I	S

191

W	A	N	T
I	N	C	H
L	U	A	U
E	T	A	S

192

S	T	O	P
C	A	B	O
A	M	O	R
M	E	E	K

193

F	L	E	A
O	I	L	S
R	I	S	K
D	I	E	S

194

S	H	O	T
T	A	K	E
A	L	A	S
T	O	Y	S

195

P	E	S	T
L	A	I	R
U	C	L	A
S	H	O	P

196

P	I	T	A
O	N	E	S
U	T	A	H
R	O	L	E

197

C	O	R	K
O	V	E	N
W	A	N	E
S	L	O	E

198

G	A	L	S
R	U	I	N
A	R	E	A
B	A	N	G

199

B	A	L	L
A	S	I	A
R	A	M	S
S	P	O	T

200

F	O	U	R
A	L	T	O
T	E	E	S
S	O	P	S

Can't get enough of *USA TODAY* puzzles?

You can play more *USA TODAY* puzzles:

- In your daily *USA TODAY* newspaper
- On USATODAY.com at puzzles.usatoday.com
- On mobile phones (certain puzzles only–check with your individual carrier)